Caledonian MacBrayne

Hebridean & Clyde Ferries

the fleet

Ian McCrorie

Published by:
Ferry Publications, PO Box 33, Ramsey, Isle of Man IM99 4LP
Tel: +44 (0) 1624 898445   Fax: +44 (0) 1624 898449 E-mail: ferrypubs@manx.net   Website: www.ferrypubs.co.uk

A Brief History

Caledonian MacBrayne Ltd was formed on 1st January 1973 when The Caledonian Steam Packet Company Ltd was renamed on taking over most of the shipping services of David MacBrayne Ltd. Both companies had very different histories.

THE ERA OF DAVID HUTCHESON & CO

The name MacBrayne had been associated with steamship services on the west coast of Scotland since 10th February 1851. In that year Messrs G & J Burns sold the goodwill of their West Highland trade and the associated ships to their Chief Clerk, David Hutcheson, on condition that one of the partners in the new firm was their nephew David MacBrayne. The third was Hutcheson's brother Alexander. With no railways in the area and roads little more than dirt tracks, the main thrust of the new company's service was from Glasgow to the mainland towns of Oban, Fort William and Inverness via the Crinan and Caledonian Canals. The only two islands included in the network were Mull and Skye.

Encouraged by the fact that Queen Victoria herself had sailed in the area in 1847, Hutcheson christened his main service "The Royal Route" and very soon, thanks to the Postmaster General, he was able to call his ships 'Royal Mail Steamers'.

The services the company offered with their eight ships were twofold. Certain steamers sailed all the way from Glasgow through the Crinan Canal or round the Mull of Kintyre to the west coast ports. The old paddlers which had been inherited were gradually replaced by screw steamers and the Hutcheson empire expanded. By 1853, Stornoway, the

*The **Columba** (1878) approaches Dunoon.*

capital of the Isle of Lewis, had become an important destination and soon more and more islands were brought into the sphere of operations, served by well-loved ships like the *Clydesdale* and *Clansman*.

Other ships, known as 'swift steamers', carried an ever-increasing number of tourists to places made famous in art, music and literature like Staffa, with its spectacular caves and rock formations, Iona, a place of pilgrimage with its ancient ruined abbey and Loch Coruisk, with the high Cuillins of Skye towering above. Ships such as the *Mountaineer*, *Iona*,

Gondolier and *Chevalier* became household names.

David Hutcheson himself retired after 25 years and, with his brother following in his footsteps shortly afterwards, David MacBrayne became sole partner. Already 65 years of age, he carried on the firm in his own name for another quarter of a century. Hutcheson was so highly thought of by the people whose transport needs he had served so well that he is commemorated by a monument on the island of Kerrera which shelters Oban Bay.

The paddle steamer *Columba* of 1878 never left the Clyde but remained for almost sixty years on MacBrayne's prestige route – the daily service at seven o'clock from Glasgow to Dunoon, Rothesay, the Kyles of Bute, Tarbert and Ardrishaig. She was arguably the greatest Clyde steamer of all time but for many years was virtually the only representative of the MacBrayne passenger fleet to ply on the Firth; in other years she had one or two consorts at most. For the history of the vast majority of Clyde steamers one has to look elsewhere.

THE EARLY DAYS OF RAILWAY STEAMERS ON THE CLYDE

For almost thirty years after the pioneer steamship *Comet* first sailed down the Clyde in 1812, travellers to the Firth's towns and villages sailed from the Broomielaw in the heart of Glasgow. It was not until 1841 that a viable alternative came into being. In that year the Glasgow & Greenock Railway opened its line along the south bank of the river, terminating at Greenock Cathcart Street station (now Greenock Central). A few minutes' walk, admittedly along one of the less salubrious streets of the town, took travellers to the Steamboat Quay: the concept of the railhead was born.

Traffic on the line rapidly grew and train connection services soon ate into the traffic of the 'all-the-way' steamers. In 1851 the Caledonian Railway, one of Scotland's major companies and popularly known as the 'Caley', took over the route and Greenock soon became the Caley's main outlet for the developing tourist and commuter trade, although the company relied on the various independent steamship owners to supply the connections. It was at this time that the main expansion of the Clyde Coast communities took place as daily travel to and from the city became

Wemyss Bay station with its floral decorations.

ever easier.

A new railway line opened to Wemyss Bay, a few miles down the coast from Greenock, in 1865. Worked by the Caledonian, it was ideally suited for the Rothesay and Millport routes. The Caledonian now carried nearly all of the rail-borne traffic to the Clyde's main resorts. Four years later, however, one of their main competitors, the Glasgow & South Western Railway Company (G&SWR), obtained access to the coast with a new line to Greenock Prince's Pier. A mile or so west of the Caley terminus, and offering direct access from station to pier, the new line became instantly popular and Caley receipts plummeted. The Caledonian quickly bought over the harbour at the little village of Gourock, a further three miles seaward of their rival's terminus, but another fifteen years were to elapse before they could take advantage of their new acquisition.

THE GOLDEN AGE OF THE CLYDE PADDLE STEAMER

In an exceptionally bold move, the Caledonian dug a tunnel 1.5 miles long – the longest in Scotland – under Greenock's West End and used the excavated material to infill part of the seafront near its exit at Gourock Bay. The railway line swept over the 'new' land, terminating in a fine station, while a new pier, nearly half a mile long, was constructed on the shoreline. The whole scheme took three years to complete and it was not until 1st June 1889 that the first commercial train steamed into Gourock Station. Overnight, Gourock was transformed from a sleepy burgh into a bustling railhead. The Caley had meanwhile bought out one of the existing steamboat operators on the Firth and so became the owner of two paddle

*The **Chevalier** (1866) (left) and **Claymore** (1882) pictured at Oban North Pier.*

steamers. They did not, however, have any powers actually to run them and they would not get Parliamentary approval to do so. On 8th May 1889, then, The Caledonian Steam Packet Co Ltd (CSP) was registered to take over all of the railway's marine activities. Thus the Clyde's premier steamer company was born. Two new paddle steamers were soon commissioned and the G&SWR were left to lick their wounds, with their rival's new headquarters at Gourock completely eclipsing their base at Prince's Pier.

Late in 1889 the Caledonian bought out the private shareholders of the

Wemyss Bay line (which they already operated) and in the following year, thanks to some audacious strategic planning on the part of their Marine Superintendent, Captain James Williamson, they placed two new vessels on the connecting services. The Caley extended their initial triumph down the Firth that year when they built a crack paddle steamer, the *Duchess of Hamilton*, to sail from a new railhead at Ardrossan to Arran. The old privately-owned steamer on the run in connection with the G&SWR trains over the long-established railway was completely outclassed.

The G&SWR hit back. Eventually securing Parliamentary permission to own their own steamers (with certain restrictions) and with Captain James's brother Alex Williamson as Marine Superintendent, the railway company produced three magnificent paddle steamers for the 1892 season. The third of these was the *Glen Sannox* which at 20.5 knots on trial was the fastest ship on the Clyde: the tables were turned when she was placed on the Arran station to win back traffic lost to the '*Hamilton*'.

Virtually every year new ships were added to the Clyde fleet and so the competition grew more intense. When the Caley added the aesthetic wonder *Duchess of Rothesay,* the G&SWR responded with the *Jupiter* and then the larger and even faster *Juno*. Even the North British Steam Packet Company (NB), which had led a somewhat humdrum existence operating out of Craigendoran on the North Bank of the river, entered the fray and produced some winners, rising to a crescendo with the *Waverley* of 1899 which could take on all comers, with the possible exception of the *Glen Sannox*.

Without doubt the 1890s were the 'high noon' of the Clyde paddle

*A CSP advert illustrating the **Duchess of Argyll** with the Arran hills in the background.*

steamer and the fleet was famed throughout the land. It has to be said that, although the Caledonian Steam Packet had the best strategic site for the coast traffic, by the close of the nineteenth century, at least at the top end of the scale, their ships were simply outclassed by their rivals.

THE COMING OF THE RAILWAY IN THE WEST HIGHLANDS

Meanwhile, the David MacBrayne West Highland fleet continued to evolve, albeit in a different way from the railway steamers. In the MacBrayne story too, the coming of the railway had a prominent place. In

1880, two years after the commissioning of the *Columba*, the Callander & Oban Railway won through to the west coast at Oban. MacBrayne initially saw this as a threat to the age-old Royal Route but in fact it turned out to be a boon, generating extra traffic to such an extent that he was able to upgrade his Oban fleet by bringing the crack steamer *Iona* round from the Clyde, displacing one of his older ships.

There was another, more far-reaching result, namely the concept of the steamer based on one of the Hebridean islands sailing in, usually daily, to the railhead with passengers, cargo and mail and returning later in the day. These new mail services supplemented the weekly or bi-weekly voyages of the all-the-way steamers from the Clyde, which slowly began to concentrate on carrying cargo rather than passengers. One ship, for example, berthed overnight at Tobermory, capital of Mull, and sailed each morning for Oban. MacBrayne based another mail steamer at Portree in Skye and took over from the Highland Railway the daily service to Strome Ferry in Loch Carron. At the same time he supplanted the local operator of the Stornoway-Ullapool mail steamer and soon transferred the mainland terminal also to the railhead at Strome Ferry. A year or two prior to this he had taken over the crossing from Islay to West Loch Tarbert, connecting here not with a train but with the *Columba* or other steamer for Glasgow.

By the end of the 1880s, mail steamers had even ventured as far as the Outer Isles. One steamer carried on a service between Skye, Harris and North Uist, not too different from that operated by Caledonian MacBrayne (CalMac) a century later. Two more were based at Oban and sailed to Coll, Tiree, Barra and the Uists, again the precursor of the present-day service. The final mail service to get under way was in 1892 when a small screw steamer commenced sailing thrice-weekly from Oban to Coll, Tiree and the west of Mull.

Two notable ships had appeared in the eighties, the noble screw steamer *Claymore*, commissioned on the all-year-round all-the-way service between Glasgow and Stornoway, and the swift steamer *Grenadier,* built for the premier day excursion from Oban to Staffa and Iona.

MacBrayne did not have the capital of the wealthy railway companies behind him and so, while the Clyde was enjoying a decade of improvement – and ruinous competition – in the nineties, he had to content himself with buying second-hand tonnage to keep his services intact and effect modest improvements. His fleet was like a museum of veterans and was a paradise for the steamer enthusiast of the day. He was able, however, to respond adequately to the advancing railways, lines to Fort William, Kyle of Lochalsh and Mallaig being opened between 1894 and 1901.

EDWARDIAN TWILIGHT

It was in 1902 that the 88-year-old David MacBrayne at last admitted his two sons, David Hope and Laurence, into full partnership with him. A change in attitude was soon observed as new tonnage was ordered for the first time in fifteen years; in fact seven new ships were commissioned in the next three years. Without the gilt and fine lines of the ships of the past, they were functional, utilitarian but economical and served the company well. Prominent among them were the *Sheila* for Stornoway and the *Clydesdale* and paddle steamer *Pioneer* for Islay.

On 1st January 1906 a private limited company was incorporated with David Hope as Chairman. The old man himself retired at the same time although he retained his 50% shareholding and visited the office daily until his death a year later, at the ripe old age of 92. He left behind him a reputation second to none in the West Highlands.

On the Clyde, the main event of the start of the new century was the coming of a new type of ship – the turbine steamer. A syndicate formed by the eminent engineer Charles Parsons, the shipbuilders Denny of Dumbarton and Captain John Williamson, another brother of Captain James, built the first commercial steamer to incorporate the new-fangled machinery. The white-funnelled *King Edward* appeared in 1901 and an improved version, the *Queen Alexandra*, the following year. The company to suffer most was the new David MacBrayne Ltd, as the new, fast, smooth and revolutionary ships sailed daily to Kintyre and Loch Fyne, in competition with the paddlers on the Royal Route. There was little MacBrayne's could do, although increasing the frequency of the Ardrishaig run did have limited success.

The CSP did not respond immediately but continued with their policy of fleet expansion by commissioning more paddle steamers, one of which, the graceful *Duchess of Fife*, did much to restore their fortunes in the Upper Firth. The only way, however, to displace the *Glen Sannox* from her position of pre-eminence on the Arran route was to embrace the new

The CSP turbine steamer **Duchess of Montrose** *(1930).*

technology. Denny's built the turbine steamer *Duchess of Argyll* for the company in 1906 and when she took her place at Ardrossan, Caley supremacy was at last restored. She was, however, the last new CSP steamer to be built for almost a quarter of a century. The railway companies were starting to reap the consequences of their profligacy. Dividends fell sharply and two CSP ships had to be withdrawn. Even this did not satisfy the shareholders and from 1909 certain receipts were shared and certain services pooled, major vessels of each fleet being laid up as a result in alternate summers. The yellow funnels of the Caledonian boats were seen for the first time, for example, at Prince's Pier, while the red and black of the G&SW appeared at Gourock and other railheads.

On the other hand, MacBrayne's in this period up to the Great War added eleven ships to their fleet of which six were new-builds. In addition they introduced their first omnibus, to run between Fort William and North Ballachulish, thus heralding the eventual replacement of certain mainland sea routes by road transport. Further daring entrepreneurial management produced three ships propelled by the new-fangled internal combustion engine, fuelled, at least initially, by paraffin. One of them, the *Lochinvar* of 1908, survived for over fifty years, mainly as the Mull mail steamer. Only one of the new ships was a paddle steamer, the *Mountaineer*, and she turned out to be the last in a long line.

Britain declared war on Germany on 4th August 1914. It was almost a year before the effects were felt keenly on the Clyde and in the West Highlands. An anti-submarine boom was erected between the Cloch and Dunoon and Clyde services were partitioned, the Royal Route starting and finishing at Wemyss Bay. By now a Shipping Controller, under Admiralty restrictions, oversaw a joint service on the Clyde. Paddle steamers, however, with their shallow draught, made successful minesweepers and nearly all the Clyde pleasure steamers were 'called up'. Some, notably the CSP's *Duchess of Hamilton* and *Duchess of Montrose*, were lost in action. West Highland services meanwhile were pared to the absolute minimum and so some of the MacBrayne veterans were available to cover the essential railway connection services on the Clyde. MacBrayne's too suffered war losses.

The Clyde's only three-funnelled steamer - **Saint Columba**.

THE AFTERMATH OF WAR

It was a depleted service that was offered in 1919 and even in 1920. The twenties and early thirties brought hard times to Britain, thanks to the memory of war deaths, inflation, industrial unrest culminating in the General Strike of 1926 and then the Wall Street Crash heralding in the Great Depression. The CSP and MacBrayne fleets fared differently. On the Clyde competition as in Victorian and Edwardian times had not really returned and when, by Act of Parliament, the individual railway companies were incorporated into new giants like the London, Midland & Scottish Railway (LMS) it was logical that their subsidiary steamer fleets should also be joined.

On 1st July 1923, then, the CSP and G&SW steamers were absorbed into the LMS Railway Company (the NB similarly being subsumed by the London & North Eastern Railway – the LNER). That season the steamers' funnels were painted a combination of the colours of the two amalgamating fleets but by 1925 standard buff funnels with black tops were finally adopted. The only new tonnage in the twenties was a turbine replacement for the *Glen Sannox* on the Arran run. She was given the same name and was virtually a repeat of the *Duchess of Argyll* built almost twenty years before, this being evidence of a lack of fresh ideas on the part of the Marine Department. In the agreement CSP vessels were still registered as such but G&SW ships were now owned directly by the LMS. The new ship, being a direct G&SW replacement, was therefore, at least initially, not a CSP vessel.

The MacBrayne vessels, admittedly operating a depleted service, also suffered from lack of finance, compounded by the fact that many of the ships were ancient and the new ones not built to the standards of the old. The Directors' suffering culminated in the *annus horribilis* of 1927 when three ships were lost by stranding or fire, most notably the swift steamer *Grenadier*. The following year David Hope MacBrayne felt obliged to withdraw the company's tender for the mail contract and a rescue package had to be devised to maintain the lifeline services to the isles. The Chairman and Managing Director of Coast Lines, together with the President of the LMS, agreed jointly to acquire the fleet and goodwill of the company, which was duly renamed, temporarily, David MacBrayne (1928) Ltd. No longer was a member of the MacBrayne family part of the management team.

Further cuts ensued and road transport, by omnibus and now also by lorry, took the place of some steamer services. Gradually ships which did not match the standards expected of a discerning public were withdrawn and replaced by vessels built under the new mail contract which had been negotiated. The first of these was the *Lochness*, built for the Stornoway mail service. She was to be the last steamship actually built for MacBrayne's but, unlike the other steamers in the Clyde and West Highlands, she burned oil rather than coal. The next two ships, the *Lochearn* and *Lochmor*, were sisters: they were motor ships powered by diesel oil. Though slow for the long voyage across the Sea of the Hebrides to the Outer Isles, they brought a new standard of comfort to the service. The last contract vessel was truly revolutionary – Britain's first diesel-electric passenger ship, the *Lochfyne* of 1931, destined for Iona in summer and the Clyde in winter. So successful was she that a second similar vessel, the *Lochnevis*, was built for the Portree mail service three years later.

THE SECOND WORLD WAR – BEFORE AND AFTER

On the Clyde, progress was managed differently. The LMS/CSP Marine Department continued to rely on the traditional coal-fired turbine or paddle steamer, coal still being a cheap commodity and its transport a vital part of railway revenues. Despite the Depression, a new turbine steamer was built in 1930 specifically for cruising. This was the second *Duchess of Montrose* and she incorporated the latest design piloted by the white-funnelled turbine *King George V* (1926) in that she had an enclosed promenade deck – but in addition she was the first single-class steamer on the river. She was so popular that a sister ship, the *Duchess of Hamilton*, was ordered two years later. By now the original CSP fleet was beginning to show its age and for the rest of the thirties a fleet replacement programme for the 'ferry-class' paddlers was the main priority. All of the new-builds bar one, the turbine *Marchioness of Graham*, were paddlers, notable among them being the *Caledonia* and *Jupiter*. To reflect the popularity of the turbine, however, they had their paddles disguised and enclosed to give the appearance of being turbine steamers themselves.

The railway steamers ran in connection with the trains from Glasgow. Operating from the heart of the city, by now from Bridge Wharf on the south side of the river, was a fleet of white-funnelled ships, two turbines and three paddlers, owned by Williamson-Buchanan Steamers Ltd. In October 1935 they were purchased by the LMS, the survivors being subsequently transferred to CSP ownership. Thus the two turbines, the pioneer *King Edward* and the new *Queen Mary II*, came into the railway fleet. The associated ships of Turbine Steamers Ltd were at the same time bought by MacBrayne's. The *King George V* took up the Staffa and Iona sailings from Oban while the *Queen Alexandra*, second of the name, was transformed, *inter alia*, by the fitting of a third (dummy) funnel and a mainmast. This allowed the company, albeit with great regret, to withdraw the much-loved *Columba* and *Iona*, the latter after seventy years of service. The name of the '*Alexandra*' was changed, most appropriately, to

Saint Columba and she proved to be a worthy successor to the great paddler on the Royal Route. Meanwhile the CSP took over the turbine routes to Campbeltown and Inveraray.

Unlike in 1914, the declaration of war on 3rd September 1939 had an immediate effect on shipping services both on the Clyde and in the Western Isles. All vessels donned battleship grey, operations were controlled by the Ministry of War Transport and several ships in both fleets were immediately requisitioned. Not only at Cloch-Dunoon but also in the Kylerhea Narrows between Mallaig and Kyle, anti-submarine booms were erected, thus making timetabling difficult. All cruising ceased. On the Clyde, essential services were largely maintained by turbines but the two MacBrayne turbines were taken over by the Admiralty, the *King George V* being among the flotilla at the evacuation of Dunkirk. As in the Great War, several ships did not return or, if they survived, were not fit for further service.

It was a depleted fleet, then, which operated the Clyde services in the late forties. Just as after the Great War different railway companies amalgamated, so in 1948 there was a further joining together, but this time under the aegis of the Government. On 1st January of that year the railways were nationalised and vested in a new state authority called The British Transport Commission (BTC), trading under the name 'British Railways'. The LMS and LNER fleets had come together, the distinctive red, white and black funnel colouring of the latter being lost in the process. The North Bank fleet comprised four paddlers: the veteran *Lucy Ashton* (which was withdrawn after a year), the crack cruising steamer *Jeanie*

A pleasant evening scene with the **Waverley** *(1947) and the* **Queen Mary II** *(1933) at Dunoon.*

Deans, the experimental diesel-electric *Talisman* and a new *Waverley*. The three remaining ships were at last legally transferred to the CSP in 1951. The integration of the two fleets took many years to come to fruition but the Craigendoran paddlers soon called at Gourock *en route* to Dunoon and Rothesay and even took over some of the former LMS winter rosters.

MODERNISATION OF A NATIONALISED FLEET

Problems abounded. There was an imbalance in the fleet with a preponderance of expensive turbines thanks to the war. Coal was costly and of poor quality, wage inflation was rampant, road transport was ever more prominent, people were going farther afield for holidays and car travel was on the increase, especially after the de-rationing of petrol. Management bit the bullet in the early fifties and embraced the culture of the motor ship, known to MacBrayne's for half a century. In 1953 a quartet of smallish diesel passenger ships, the 'Maids', appeared on the scene. They were innovatory, functional rather than opulent, slower than the ships they replaced but much, much cheaper to operate, thanks to lower fuel costs and smaller crews. Despite not receiving the mark of approval from the traditionalists, their comfort was appreciated, especially by winter travellers. There had been motor vessels in the fleet since the late 1930s but they were much smaller.

The true revolution, however, came the following year with the arrival of three car ferries, affectionately known as the 'ABC ferries' after their names, *Arran*, *Bute* and *Cowal*. Each of the diesel vessels sported an electrically-operated hoist aft of the passenger accommodation that allowed vehicles to be loaded at all states of the tide. No longer did intrepid drivers have to board by way of unsteady and unprotected wooden planks. The new 'dual-purpose vessels', as they were called, could accommodate around 30 cars and 650 passengers as they crossed between Gourock and Dunoon and Wemyss Bay and Rothesay. Turnrounds were slow at low tide and the passenger complement low for peak times: there was still a role for the conventional steamer at such periods. The last hoist-loading CSP car ferry, the *Glen Sannox*, was commissioned in 1957, appropriately for the Arran run. She was an enlarged and improved version of the pioneering trio, being able to carry

*The **Caledonia** and the **Columba** off Craignure, Mull.*

1,100 passengers and up to 50 cars. Traffic on all three routes increased by leaps and bounds and the ferries were hard pressed to cope in the busy season. Meanwhile, during the decade seven of the favourite older steamers had been withdrawn.

With the CSP name and colours now prominent, the extensive programme of excursions and ferry crossings continued, despite increasing losses and deteriorating weather. During the Beeching era in railway history it would have been surprising if the axe had not eventually fallen but two of the best-loved ships from the thirties, the *Duchess of Montrose* and *Jeanie Deans*, were laid up after the 1964 season and the cruising programme was reduced. Replaced herself by a smaller vessel, one of the 'Maids' later took over from the DEPV *Talisman*, which by that time was serving Millport. As a result, in the last year of the decade, only four actual steamships remained in service. Incidentally, since 1965, the CSP ships, in line with other vessels owned by British Railways, had their hulls painted 'monastral' blue. A degree of autonomy remained, however, with the retention of the buff funnel, now emblazoned proudly with the Caley lion.

CAR FERRIES TO THE HEBRIDES

The West Highlands had to wait for ten years longer than the Clyde before the car ferry revolution was initiated. Three new conventional mail 'steamers' had taken up their stations since the outbreak of war – the *Lochiel* on the Islay station in 1940, the long-awaited Stornoway mailboat *Loch Seaforth* in late 1947 and the modern-looking *Claymore* on the 'Inner Isles run' from Oban in 1955. In 1948 not only had David MacBrayne Ltd experienced nationalisation when the LMS 50% holding was transferred to the BTC, but they had also taken over the fleet of their friendly rivals McCallum, Orme & Co Ltd. This firm had for many years operated a complementary network of sailings to different parts of the Western Isles and now many islands previously not served by MacBrayne's came into the company's orbit. The most distinguished vessel to be transferred was the much-loved *Hebrides* of 1898. Around this period there was a retrenchment in the provision of all-the-way sailings from the Clyde, now carrying almost exclusively cargo and heavy goods. New ships replaced old and many of the age-old routes were combined or, in some cases, replaced by road transport. The company now owned over a hundred buses.

One area which was already provided with vehicle ferries was the short crossing from Kyle of Lochalsh to Kyleakin in Skye, operated by the CSP. By the late fifties so little traffic went on the alternative route via the

Caledonian MacBrayne's **Clansman** *and* **Columba** *pictured at Oban.*

Lochnevis to Portree that MacBrayne's, after trying unsuccessfully to withdraw the service completely, eventually purchased a smaller vessel – a wooden inshore minesweeper renamed *Loch Arkaig* – to keep the route open for a few years. The *Lochnevis* herself moved to Oban, the Oban excursion vessel *Lochfyne* was based permanently on the Clyde and the favourite turbine steamer *Saint Columba* was withdrawn in 1958.

The year 1964 saw the coming of the car ferry at last. Finance was provided for the ingenious expedient, allowed by a new Act of Parliament, of having the ships built for the Secretary of State for Scotland and chartered to MacBrayne's. First came the *Hebrides* on the route from a fully-renovated pier at Uig in the north of Skye to Tarbert, Harris, and Lochmaddy in North Uist, the latter island now joined by causeway to Benbecula and South Uist. A second ferry, the *Clansman*, sailed between Mallaig and Armadale in the south of Skye, where a much-improved road system connected with Uig, while a third, the *Columba*, linked Oban with a completely new pier at Craignure in Mull and Lochaline in Morvern. The three ships could carry 50 cars and 600 passengers but in addition they were fitted out with 50 sleeping berths. This was because tourists and their cars were targeted more than cargo, which still arrived in the isles direct by sea from Glasgow. The mailboats from Oban, Mallaig and Kyle were withdrawn and small vessels commissioned to serve the islands which would otherwise be bypassed. It is significant in view of future events that there was no provision initially for a dual-purpose vessel to serve Islay and the other islands in the south.

THE MOMENTOUS EVENTS OF THE EARLY STG YEARS

A hugely significant event occurred on 1st January 1969 when the Scottish Transport Group (STG) was created by the Government. The CSP, removed from railway control after eighty years, became a wholly-owned subsidiary, along with the dominant Scottish Bus Group. In addition, the STG acquired the 50% holding in MacBrayne's from British Railways and on 1st July purchased the remaining half-share held by Coast Lines. For the first time David MacBrayne Ltd was wholly nationalised. Their buses and lorries were transferred to other subsidiaries. The most immediate tangible result was the withdrawal of some of the

oldest ships. A MacBrayne vessel operating in CSP territory was now anomalous: after continuous operation since 1851, the service from Gourock to Ardrishaig soon ceased and the *Lochfyne* placed on the sale list. The expensive though popular cruise paddler *Caledonia* was also laid up after the 1969 season, as was the even more celebrated turbine *Duchess of Hamilton* the following year.

One of the first problems with which the STG had to deal was Islay. While progress towards a car ferry for the route was stalled for political reasons, a private company, Western Ferries, had stepped in with a no-frills service with utilitarian ships and terminals and had taken a fair amount of traffic from MacBrayne's. After a stop-gap solution using two conventional ships, MacBrayne's had proposed to counter with a purpose-built car ferry for the route operating from a new terminal in deep water some miles down the loch from West Loch Tarbert Pier, but this plan had been thwarted when the site was refused by the local authority. Shrewdly, the STG decided to relocate the pioneer CSP car ferry *Arran* to the route as her smaller size allowed her to use the existing terminals, while the new-build could be commissioned on the Clyde and give much-needed extra capacity to the Dunoon route. This indeed happened in 1970, with the *Arran* resplendent in MacBrayne red and black and the new *Iona* in CSP yellow. Two passenger and two cargo vessels were withdrawn in consequence.

The main strategic problem facing the STG, however, was how to cater for the ever-increasing levels of vehicle traffic and size of commercial vehicles and coaches on the roads. Fashions were changing and freight

*A winter scene with the **Glen Sannox** in CalMac colours.*

companies now preferred their cargo carried in lorries which could then be taken to the island destination without trans-shipment. Hoist-loading was slow and the only way forward was the initially expensive option of constructing linkspans at the various terminals and building or modifying ships to operate a roll on-roll off system. The guinea pig was the Arran route. Linkspans were indeed installed at Ardrossan Harbour and Brodick Pier and the STG bought from Stena Line a Swedish ferry fitted with bow and stern doors to allow drive-through operation. She was given the name *Caledonia* and entered service in May 1970.

The *Glen Sannox*, complete with a new stern ramp so that she could relieve on the Arran station, was transferred initially to Rothesay with further 'musical chairs' resulting. The CSP also started to operate small bow-loading ferries, taking over the operation of the ferries on the 'back door' to Bute between Colintraive and Rhubodach and launching a new service between Largs and Cumbrae as the main communication to the island. Turntable ferries, which had been on the Skye crossing between Kyle and Kyleakin, had been made redundant on the commissioning of two larger drive on-drive off ferries, the *Kyleakin* and *Lochalsh*. They were transferred to the Clyde and duly modified to take up these routes. The Kintyre peninsula was kept in the network following the withdrawal of the MacBrayne steamer first by a short-lived car ferry service from Fairlie to Tarbert via Brodick but more permanently when a new small bow-loader was introduced in 1972. Appropriately named *Kilbrannan*, she was the first of several 'Island' class ferries to be built and was placed on a new and very successful seasonal service across the Kilbrannan Sound from Lochranza in North Arran to Claonaig, a few miles south of Tarbert in Kintyre.

Meanwhile the STG were urgently considering replacing the mailboat *Loch Seaforth* on the Stornoway run with a drive-through service. As a stopgap the *Iona* was given a MacBrayne red funnel and transferred north, with the *Glen Sannox* replacing her at Dunoon. She still ran from Kyle of Lochalsh despite the longer passage time but plans were laid to transfer the mainland terminal to Ullapool to give the shortest sea crossing. Appropriate linkspans were installed and the car ferry *Clansman* modified from hoist-loading to drive-through operation so that she could operate the service.

CALEDONIAN MACBRAYNE LTD

While all these significant changes both on the Clyde and in the Western Isles were taking place, the two companies operating under the Scottish Transport Group umbrella were being edged closer and closer together. It therefore came as no surprise when, on 1st January 1973, they actually merged, The Caledonian Steam Packet Co Ltd being renamed Caledonian MacBrayne Ltd and taking over the shipping services of the CSP and the major MacBrayne routes. The corollary was that Clyde as well as West Highland services were subject to Government subsidy. David MacBrayne Ltd (which remained in existence) was retained to operate other mail and cargo services and small vessels for a few years, but the whole operation was managed by Caledonian MacBrayne. Gourock became the headquarters of the 'new' company, although complete integration took a considerable time, the personnel of the two divisions, for example, remaining in different trade unions. The road haulage services that were now operated by a separate company under the STG were sold by the Government in 1985.

A substantial part of the subsequent history of Caledonian MacBrayne, or CalMac as it soon came to be called, can be gleaned from the stories of the individual ships.

The unsubsidised competition on the Islay route was seen off first of all by transforming the *Arran* into a stern-loading vessel and then in 1974 by commissioning a new vessel for the route, the *Pioneer*. The converted *Clansman* duly took up the Stornoway-Ullapool service but, as she was somewhat under-powered, she had to be replaced in the long term. A ship already building in Norway for another company was bought by CalMac, named *Suilven* after a prominent mountain and placed on the route across the Minch, also in 1974. Being able to carry 120 cars, she solved any capacity problems at a stroke. The old Stornoway boat *Loch Seaforth* had in 1973 been transferred to Oban to increase capacity on the 'Inner Isles Mail run'. She had come to grief, however, after a short period when she struck a rock in the Gunna Sound between Coll and Tiree and subsequently sank at Tiree Pier. She was only fit for breaking up and the ship she had replaced, the *Claymore*, had to return to the fray. With new linkspans in place at Oban and Craignure, Mull, a drive-through ferry had to be dedicated to that route to supersede the hoist-loading *Columba*. The *Iona*, no longer needed at Stornoway, was the ideal candidate. That was how the *Clansman* was replaced at Mallaig after she had been

*The **Arran** and MacBrayne buses at Port Ellen, Islay.*

converted - her sister *Columba*, redundant at Oban, was able to succeed her.

Meanwhile Western Ferries had started an opposition service to what was then one of CalMac's busiest routes – Gourock-Dunoon. They operated two basic roll on-roll off ferries between simple terminals at McInroy's Point and Hunter's Quay and, as at Islay, won a fair proportion of the traffic. The appearance of the new *Jupiter* and *Juno* – so manoeuvrable that they became affectionately known as 'streakers' – helped stem Western Ferries' advance for some time. Their arrival in 1974 allowed the *Glen Sannox* to move round to Oban for the Mull service. The *Iona* could then be spared to inaugurate a new 'marine motorway' from

Oban to Castlebay, Barra, and Lochboisdale, South Uist. Initially the vessel had to use her hoist but eventually both island terminals had linkspans installed. As it happened, the *Glen Sannox* did not remain long on summer sailings in the Western Isles because on the appearance of the *Suilven* at Stornoway, her predecessor, the *Clansman*, went on to the Oban-Mull station. The *'Sannox'* returned to the Clyde and displaced the *Bute* (one of the original Clyde car ferries) from the Rothesay route. The latter was modified for employment on the Mallaig-Armadale crossing and her appearance there in time for the 1975 season allowed the *Columba* to return to Oban. There she took over both the Coll and Tiree sailings and the age-old day excursion to Iona, albeit on a reduced frequency. That is why the veteran turbine *King George V* could be withdrawn, a real heartbreak for her thousands of devotees. Meanwhile, with more and more routes being transferred to ro-ro operation, the need for a cargo service all the way from Glasgow grew less and less. Eventually, in late 1976, the last of the cargo boats, the *Loch Carron*, was withdrawn, thus bringing to an end a tradition lasting 125 years.

This left the turbine *Queen Mary II* as the only 'real' steamer left in either the Clyde or West Highland fleet. Since 1971 she had been employed mainly on day excursions from Gourock, as pleasure sailings from Glasgow down the Clyde had by then ceased. For the first three years she had worked in tandem with the paddle steamer *Waverley* but CalMac then decided, reluctantly, that essential reboilering for the paddler was too expensive and they were compelled to withdraw her. Magnanimously, they donated her to the Paddle Steamer Preservation

*The **Suilven** (1974) at Stornoway while on the Ullapool service.*

Society for the princely sum of one pound. It could not have been predicted at the time that more than thirty five years on she would still be sailing 'doon the watter', as fine a ship as the day she was built, thanks to Heritage Lottery money and a great deal of dedication. The turbine lasted three more years, but competing with 'the last sea-going paddle steamer in the world' proved to be an uneven struggle and she was withdrawn after the 1977 season.

By the following year the *Saturn* had appeared on the Rothesay-Wemyss Bay station, with both terminals equipped with linkspans, and the *Glen Sannox*, which had previously been re-engined, refurbished and upgraded, took over the mantle of Clyde cruise steamer. She was employed as a car ferry at weekends and peak periods but, despite this seemingly sensible economic approach, she continued to lose money and in 1981 she retired from that role. Historically the railway companies were also involved in pleasure sailings on Loch Lomond. At this period, one paddle steamer remained, the *Maid of the Loch*, managed by CalMac, but again for economic reasons she was also withdrawn in 1981.

While all this activity was taking place regarding the main routes to the main islands, a quiet revolution was also to be seen on a smaller scale. Following the success of the CSP's *Kilbrannan* (1972) on the 'back door' to Arran, a further seven 'Island' class vessels were commissioned by 1976, of which two remain in CalMac service. The islands served by these small bow-loading ferries included Mull (from Lochaline in Morvern), Iona, Gigha, Scalpay, Raasay and Lismore. The frequency of sailings to all the islands increased appreciably. Cumbrae was served by two older bow-loaders which were proving inadequate but when the larger drive-through ferry *Isle of Cumbrae* appeared in 1977, difficulties were quickly resolved. Capacity problems were also evident on the main route to Arran from Ardrossan but these were solved by the simple expedient of switching the *Caledonia* and the larger *Clansman*. The former was able to cope – just – with the cars and passengers offering for Mull and the latter brought about a marked improvement on the Arran service.

In the last year of the decade two further developments took place. With numbers carried increasing relentlessly thanks to the modernisation of the fleet, a new stern-loading *Claymore* was commissioned for the crossing from Oban to Barra and South Uist (together with Coll and Tiree in winter). This allowed the *Iona* to move to Islay, as had been the intention ten years previously. She was able to do this as CalMac had taken over the old Western Ferries terminal at Kennacraig, where a deep-draughted vessel could berth. The previous Islay ferry *Pioneer*, complete with hoist, was switched to the Mallaig-Armadale roster, thus allowing the *Bute*, and coincidentally the other two 'ABC ferries', *Arran* and *Cowal*, to be disposed of. The other improvement was the commissioning of a purpose-built replacement for the *Loch Arkaig*, which had served the Small Isles of Eigg, Muck, Rum and Canna almost continuously since the car ferry revolution of 1964. The *Lochmor*, able to carry two cars on her open deck aft, provided a lifeline to the islands and a fine day excursion for tourists.

In the ten or so STG years until the end of the seventies, bald statistics show that eighteen ships were added to the fleet of CalMac and its predecessors, while twenty three were withdrawn and sold, either for further service or for scrap. These figures do not on their own do justice to the fact that during the period the entire service on the Clyde and in the Western Isles was revolutionised. While many long-standing traditions were axed, the frequency of sailings, the ease of travel and the increase in the point-to-point short sea routes all led to a vastly improved service. The main difference, of course, stemmed from the provision of drive-on drive-off facilities on almost all the major routes. All that remained for CalMac in the following quarter century was to complete this process and respond to the ever-increasing passenger and vehicle traffic.

*The **Pioneer** on passage in the Clyde.*

THE EIGHTIES AND NINETIES

Four major routes were improved during the eighties by the provision of new ships. The *Isle of Arran* entered service on the Arran route in 1984, allowing the slow and unwieldy *Clansman* to be sold. The following year it was the turn of the *Hebridean Isles* which, thanks to the eventual fitting of end-loading linkspans at Uig, Tarbert and Lochmaddy, brought drive-through provision to the Uig triangle. This had been one of the original ambitions of the STG and brought about significant traffic growth. The hoist-loading car ferry *Hebrides* was withdrawn. It was 1988 before the third vessel appeared: this was the *Isle of Mull*, her large capacity for both passengers and cars being a huge boost for the tourist trade to the eponymous island. She was a replacement for the *Caledonia* in summer and the *Glen Sannox* in winter and both these ships could be sold, the latter after over thirty years' yeoman service. Finally in 1989 came the *Lord of the Isles*, built to replace two ships and combine the service out of Oban to Coll and Tiree and to Barra and Lochboisdale. A new linkspan had just been installed at Castlebay, Barra, and Coll and Tiree did not have to wait too long for theirs. Considerably smaller than the *Isle of Mull*, her capacity was more than adequate at the time and her considerable speed was a much-appreciated asset. The consequent withdrawal of the *Columba* brought to an end the long-established day trip to Staffa and Iona, excursionists having to travel to Craignure and then by coach across Mull. The former Outer Isles ferry *Claymore* was then transferred to Islay, the *Iona* to Mallaig-Armadale and the *Pioneer*, minus her hoist, repaired to the Clyde.

Despite this success, the company was investigated by the Monopolies and Mergers Commission in the early eighties. Their report was generally very favourable although several recommendations were made, many of which were eventually implemented. At the same time the Westminster Government proposed to withdraw the subsidy on the Gourock-Dunoon route; by popular demand this was not accepted but the subsidy was henceforth to be for passengers only and the subsidised service was limited to one sailing per hour, except at peak times. The result was that Western Ferries' share of the car traffic gradually increased.

Meanwhile, some of the smaller islands were better catered for by the appearance of a new type of ferry – the 'Loch' class. These four double-ended 12-car ferries – *Loch Striven*, *Loch Linnhe*, *Loch Riddon* and *Loch Ranza* – replaced the smaller 'Island' class ferries on the crossings to Cumbrae, Bute (from Colintraive) and Arran (from Claonaig). The *Isle of Cumbrae* in summer and a 'Loch' class in winter likewise superseded the smaller 'Island' class on the Mull service from Lochaline.

The pattern in the nineties was very similar – three major and six 'Loch' class vessels appeared, while any remaining linkspans which were required were installed. At the very start of the decade, on 2nd April 1990, ownership of Caledonian MacBrayne Ltd was transferred to the Secretary of State for Scotland. The Government had decided to privatise the Scottish Transport Group but in the end it kept CalMac in the public sector. As in the eighties, the first substantial ferry was for Arran, the *Caledonian Isles* taking over the route in 1993, the need for such a large vessel being testament to the role played by the *Isle of Arran* in increasing traffic during her ten years on the route. The older vessel was transferred to Islay with the *Claymore* becoming spare. The second major new-build, the *Isle of Lewis*, was even more impressive with accommodation for almost a thousand passengers and 114 cars, and with a trial speed of nearly 19 knots. She took over the Stornoway-Ullapool crossing from the ageing *Suilven* in 1995. The third ferry appeared in 1998: this was the *Clansman* and she was purpose-built for the islands run from Oban in lieu of the *Lord of the Isles*, whose capacity was insufficient for the traffic she had generated on the route. The smaller ship was transferred to Mallaig

and this allowed the *Iona* to be withdrawn as she was unable to meet the new and more stringent safety regulations at reasonable cost.

As part of the agreement to build a bridge to Skye and to improve the service in the short term, two new 'Lochs' were commissioned in 1991 on the understanding that they would be sold once the bridge was completed. The *Loch Dunvegan* and *Loch Fyne* were sizeable vessels and replaced the two Skye ferries dating from the early 1970s as they could no longer cope. Four years later, when the bridge opened, their employment on the short Kyle-Kyleakin crossing came to an end as planned. They were initially placed on the sales list but after a period of idleness were re-employed as the dedicated ferries on the Colintraive and Lochaline stations respectively.

1992 brought the *Loch Buie* for Iona and the *Loch Tarbert* for Lochranza, the appearance of the latter allowing the *Loch Ranza* to be transferred to Gigha where a larger ship was also needed. In 1996 a further expansion of CalMac's activities took place. The *Loch Bhrusda* was built to provide a much-needed link between North Uist and Harris across the treacherous Sound of Harris; this allowed the Uig ferry to concentrate on shipping traffic to and from rather than between the Outer Isles. The traffic generated by the new ferry was phenomenal. Finally came the *Loch Alainn* in 1997. As the name suggests she was destined for the Lochaline-Fishnish route, but following an unfortunate debut there she was transferred to the Clyde and became the mainstay of the Largs-Cumbrae crossing. As a result of the advent of these ships, older 'Lochs' were able to replace 'Island' class ferries on the Raasay-Sconser (Skye) and

Tobermory-Kilchoan (Ardnamurchan) rosters.

Two other novel routes opened in the 1990s. The crossing at the mouth of Loch Fyne between Tarbert and Portavadie, on the Cowal peninsula, was entrusted in 1994 to an 'Island' class ferry on a seasonal basis but four years later, when more tonnage became available, a 'Loch' took over. With drive-through operation, the route, offered in winter as well as summer, was now able to reach its full potential.

In late 1996 first the *Bruernish* and then the *Canna* provided a service between Rathlin Island and Ballycastle in Northern Ireland, initially under charter but very soon in CalMac's own name. This service in a seemingly strange outpost came about as plans were mooted to inaugurate a service from Campbeltown across the channel to Ballycastle, but when no subsidy was available, CalMac under the terms of the undertaking with the Government, could not provide the service. They were in fact forced to sell the *Claymore* to a private company which used her on the route – unprofitably – for three years. In her final three years as a CalMac vessel, from 1994 until 1996, she had broken new ground by sailing between Ardrossan and Douglas, Isle of Man, at weekends during the high season. These voyages, the first CalMac sailings to be rostered outside Scotland, were in association with the Isle of Man Steam Packet Company.

A NEW MILLENNIUM

CalMac did not stand still in the new millennium but introduced various improvements to the network. First came a replacement for the *Lochmor* on the route from Mallaig to the Small Isles. The innovative *Lochnevis* took up service late in 2000 and was designed to use both the linkspans at Mallaig and Armadale and the slipways due to be constructed at each of the islands – but she still had to be able to work with flitboats in the two-year interim period.

2001 saw the coming of a new *Hebrides* which increased capacity on the Uig route to the Outer Isles by 50%. Her arrival allowed the *Hebridean Isles* to move to Islay and replace the *Isle of Arran*. She in turn became spare vessel for a year but in 2002 she gave additional services out of Oban; from 2003 she took over the role of second vessel on the Islay station at the height of the season when traffic levels justified the use of two ferries. That year also saw the completion of the project to join all the inhabited Outer Isles by causeway or ferry. By now, the island of Berneray had been linked by causeway to North Uist and Eriskay to South Uist. The *Loch Portain* was commissioned on the Sound of Harris route, sailing between Berneray and Leverburgh, Harris, and this allowed the *Loch Bhrusda* to form the last link of the chain by crossing the Sound of Barra between Barra and Eriskay. Traffic here increased so rapidly that the larger *Loch Alainn* was needed to sustain the route in 2007. One of the long-held dreams of the islanders had come to fruition.

From 2003 it was the *Lord of the Isles* which was the additional ferry based at Oban to serve mainly on the Colonsay, Tiree and Barra routes along with the *Clansman*. The *Pioneer*, whose normal summer duty by this time was merely to give peak sailings to and from Dunoon, replaced her at Mallaig. She was able to work there instead of Gourock because CalMac had chartered a catamaran, the *Ali Cat*, and she was already carrying out supplementary Dunoon crossings on a passenger-only basis. The popular *Pioneer* was withdrawn after the 2003 season and in 2004 a new, dedicated ferry, the *Coruisk*, took over the run in summer. She had actually appeared the previous year but her time on station was brief as, because of a computer failure, she had run aground and had had to be taken out of service.

From 2005 until 2007 the spotlight switched to the Clyde. The route between Wemyss Bay and Rothesay had become CalMac's busiest but it was served by two ageing 'streakers'. Upgrading was essential and came in the form of two sister ships, the *Bute* (2005) and *Argyle* (2007). Both built in Poland, they could carry almost double the number of vehicles of their predecessors and, as fast, comfortable and thoroughly modern vessels, they were a great boon both to the islanders on Bute and to the steady stream of tourists visiting the island in increasing numbers. The island of Cumbrae, too, required a ferry with larger capacity at the busiest periods. With the appearance of the *Loch Shira*, a product of Ferguson's of Port Glasgow in 2007, this objective was met and the incumbent ferry could be deployed elsewhere. To allow the new ferry to berth at Largs overnight, the ageing pier was extended and rebuilt. At the same time certain other terminals, owned either by the company or the local authority, were upgraded. Notable examples were Rothesay, Port Askaig and Oban, all of which acquired new linkspans. In the case of Rothesay, end-loading facilities were introduced for the first time, although the associated pier works were delayed and caused disruption for many months.

The **Caledonian Isles** *outward bound from Ardrossan. (Dave Wolstenholme)*

TENDERING THE ORKNEY AND SHETLAND SERVICES

On another front, CalMac, in a joint company with the Royal Bank of Scotland, responded to the invitation from the Scottish Executive to tender for lifeline services to the Northern Isles of Orkney and Shetland. As NorthLink Orkney & Shetland Ferries Ltd, they were appointed preferred bidder and eventually took over the services from P&O Scottish Ferries with a fleet of new ships in October 2002.

TENDERING THE CLYDE AND HEBRIDES FERRY SERVICES

A tendering exercise for CalMac's own network similar to that for the Northern Isles ferry services was later enforced under European Union (EU) 'State Aids' legislation. After extensive consultation, the Scottish Executive proposed a public sector owning company which would lease the existing CalMac vessels and infrastructure to operators over a five-year period. CalMac would be allowed to bid "on a fair and full cost basis". Later it was agreed with Brussels that the network should be tendered as a whole – to prevent cherry-picking of routes and to retain all the benefits of an integrated transport system – and that mainland-to-mainland routes could be included. Meanwhile, a judgment concerning a German bus company, Altmark, stated that, if a public transport company met certain criteria, that company would be exempt from the tendering process. Some legal opinion tended to agree that CalMac did meet the criteria and in December 2004 the Scottish Parliament voted by a majority of one against the Scottish Ministers' proposal to tender the Clyde and Hebrides ferry services. Following extensive consultation with the EU Commission and the UK Government, however, the Scottish Ministers concluded that they would be infringing European law if the tendering process did not continue. Accordingly, in September 2005, following further debate in the Scottish Parliament, it was confirmed that the tender process for the Clyde and Hebrides ferry services must proceed.

Following this announcement, the Scottish Ministers invited expressions of interest in tendering for the services. The press reported

*The **Argyle** crossing to Wemyss Bay. (Dave Wolstenholme)*

that there were seven interested parties, although by December that number had decreased to three – CalMac themselves, Western Ferries and V Ships, one of the world's largest ship management companies. Western Ferries withdrew in May 2006 and, in January 2007, V Ships followed suit, leaving CalMac as the only company interested in bidding. Just before this turn of events, the Scottish Transport Minister had announced the final stage of the tendering process, including the provision of additional sailings on several routes, a new £20 million ferry for Islay and consideration of a revived link between Mallaig and Lochboisdale. He also announced proposals for the return of bids for the contract by May 2007 and the selection of the preferred operator in the early summer. The bid was duly submitted by CalMac by the specified date and the new subsidy contract came into operation for a six-year period in October.

In a separate, and at the time surprise, statement, the Scottish Ministers announced that, since there was a private sector competitor on the Gourock-Dunoon route – Western Ferries – carrying most of the vehicular traffic, this route would be the subject of a separate tender for an unsubsidised service. Meanwhile, during 2004, a breakwater with end-loading linkspan had been constructed with Scottish Executive funding at the exposed Victorian pier at Dunoon. The breakwater itself was a great boon for vessels using the side-loading linkspan, but CalMac had no suitable vessels available to use the new end-loading facility. The Scottish Executive received no bids in response to its invitation to tender for the unsubsidised service, with CalMac quoting their annual loss of around £2.5 million on the route and Western Ferries referring to an 'inflexible service specification'. CalMac was therefore asked to continue using a 'streaker' on an hourly frequency until the long-term future of the 'centre-to-centre' service was decided.

The Scottish Ministers had decided that, as a requirement of the tendering process, there should be a clear legal separation between the company that operated the ferry services and the company that owned the vessels and ports. In addition, regardless of the outcome of the tendering process, the successful bidder would be expected to operate under the brand Caledonian MacBrayne. To comply with these demands, Caledonian MacBrayne Ltd had to be restructured. A new wholly-owned subsidiary, Caledonian MacBrayne Crewing (Guernsey) Ltd, had already been created to provide an offshore crewing facility. In April 2006 the company established another new wholly-owned subsidiary, CalMac Ferries Ltd (CFL), which would be used to bid for the contract for the Clyde and Hebrides ferry services. More fundamental changes were to follow. On 1st October 2006, CalMac Ferries Ltd became a subsidiary of the formerly dormant David MacBrayne Ltd which, like Caledonian MacBrayne Ltd itself, was wholly owned by the Scottish Ministers, and the operation of the Clyde and Hebrides ferry services together with the crewing company was transferred to it. The ownership of the vessels and ports continued to be vested in Caledonian MacBrayne Ltd which, in recognition of the change in its role and functions, was renamed Caledonian Maritime Assets Ltd (CMAL) and moved to Port Glasgow. From 1st October 2006, CFL, as the operators of the ferry services, leased the vessels from CMAL.

In April 2007, David MacBrayne Ltd (DML) created two further, more route-specific, subsidiary companies – Cowal Ferries Ltd to operate the service between Gourock and Dunoon (subsidised for passengers only) and Rathlin Ferries Ltd to operate the Rathlin-Ballycastle service in Northern Ireland (although the latter lost the tender in April 2008). NorthLink Ferries Ltd was already a wholly-owned subsidiary of Caledonian MacBrayne Ltd and passed to DML following the signing of a new contract and the handover of the Northern Isles ferry services on 6th July 2006. Thus the four ferry-operating companies had become part of

*The **Isle of Mull** approaching Oban Bay. (Dave Wolstenholme)*

David MacBrayne Limited, bringing to the fore again the name which is synonymous with the provision of ferry services on the west coast of Scotland. Further restructuring took place on 1st April 2009. The parent company, now known as the DML Group, was in future to address policy and strategic issues, and a number of staff who provided support in areas like finance and technical matters now worked across the Group. As a result, the Managing Director of CFL was appointed Group Chief Executive while CFL's Operations Director and NFL's Chief Executive became Managing Directors of their respective companies.

The Scottish Government, with the Scottish National Party (SNP) the majority party, have recently taken two important initiatives on Scottish ferries. A full review of all services commenced in 2008. Detailed consideration was to be given to funding, together with costs and affordability, and procurement. Each route was to be analysed and fares, ports and harbours investigated. The issue of competition would be examined, and integration with other forms of transport (e.g. railways, buses) and freight issues were considered important. A full assessment was to be made of the potential for introducing new tonnage, perhaps to include catamarans and the replacement of large ferries by two or more smaller vessels. At the same time the European Union launched a formal investigation to ensure that the whole tendering process had been compliant with the appropriate rules. They found this to be so. The EU also funded, through their inter-regional programme, an 18-month 'Small Ferries Project' in which CMAL worked with Government Departments not only in Scotland but also in Northern Ireland and the Republic of Ireland. The idea was that by procuring to a common ferry design, costs could be cut as the older generation of 'Island' and 'Loch' class ferries were replaced.

On 19th October 2008, a Road Equivalent Tariff (RET) pilot scheme got underway and was due to run until the spring of 2011. The Government hoped that by running it for well over two years its effectiveness could be fully assessed and any impact, whether positive or negative, could be identified. RET involves setting ferry fares on the basis of the cost of

*The **Lord of the Isles** and **Loch Linnhe** pass each other off Rabha nan Gall lighthouse in the Sound of Mull. (Dave Wolstenholme)*

travelling an equivalent distance by road, although it is not quite as simple as that. The relatively high cost of ferry fares had been seen as a possible barrier to economic growth on the islands. The pilot affected fares on routes from the mainland to the Outer Isles, together with Coll and Tiree. The other islands were not included – an understandable source of resentment.

FULL STEAM AHEAD

CalMac Ferries Ltd and their predecessors have been in business for over 150 years and are the proud possessors of an extensive tradition of service to the communities of the west coast of Scotland. The importance of Gaelic in this heritage is manifest in the painting of the ships' Gaelic names on their superstructures while the company shows its support for the indigenous language of the isles in many other ways. Now CalMac Ferries Ltd is a thoroughly modern company operating over thirty ships to and from twenty five different islands. Safety considerations are paramount in all its doings as are passenger needs and comfort. Marketing techniques and literature are always being improved while the ships and terminals are constantly being refurbished. Annually CalMac carry over five million passengers, one million cars, 13,000 coaches and 90,000 commercial vehicles (with a combined length of almost a million metres).

The building programme is never likely to stand still and a new purpose-built ferry for Islay is already under construction in Poland, with delivery promised for 2011. The implementation of State Aids legislation started in the autumn of 2007 and the second round of tenders for the Clyde and Hebridean services is planned for 2013. Despite all the changes, the brand name Caledonian MacBrayne will continue to feature for many years to come.

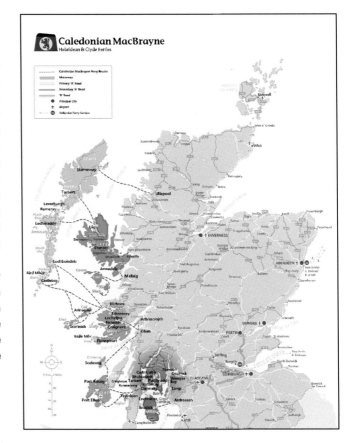

The *Isle of Arran* and *Clansman* in Tobermory Bay. (Dave Wolstenholme)

JUPITER
Iùpadar

Gourock - Dunoon

The oldest of CalMac's vessels is the *Jupiter*, purpose-built for service purely on the Upper Clyde. She was launched on 27th November 1973 by Mrs John Whittle, wife of the company's then General Manager, and first appeared on the Gourock-Dunoon crossing on 19th March 1974, replacing the *Glen Sannox*. At the time she was considered revolutionary as she was fitted with Voith-Schneider units fore and aft rather than conventional screws. These made her exceptionally manoeuvrable, which is why the *Jupiter* and her two subsequent sister ships became affectionately known as the 'streakers'. Passenger accommodation is situated forward on three decks – there are two lounges, one serving also as a bar and cafeteria.

The *Jupiter* offers an hourly-interval service on the Dunoon crossing. Vehicles board by her stern ramp at Gourock and by the starboard ramp at Dunoon. Initially she was also used to ferry Ministry of Defence (MoD) workers between Gourock and Kilcreggan and was frequently to be seen transporting gas tankers to Rothesay, the mainstay of the Dunoon service at the time being her younger sister *Juno* (still owned by CMAL but not presently chartered to CFL). In 1981 the then Secretary of State for Scotland restricted the subsidy for the Dunoon run to passengers only and CalMac was limited to one sailing per hour in case it forced the private opposition Western Ferries out of business. After modifications the *Jupiter* was given a summer passenger certificate for Arran, useful as in certain seasons between 1985 and 2000 the 'streakers' were involved in the revival of Clyde cruising. From 1986 the three ships started interchanging regularly on the Upper Firth runs. Since 2006, however, with new tonnage on the Firth, the *Jupiter* has been used exclusively on the Dunoon service. The future is uncertain, as she is now 35 years old and Dunoon Pier is in a poor state of repair. The political decision about the future cannot be long delayed.

Miles Cowsill

Gross tons	849
Length	66.45m
Breadth	13.8m
Draught	2.45m
Maximum Passenger Capacity	531
Vehicles	38
Builders	James Lamont & Co Ltd, Port Glasgow
Built	1974
Speed	12 knots
Retail Area	Coffee Cabin

Jupiter (John Newth)

SATURN
Satharn

The Wemyss Bay-Rothesay service was the last on the Clyde to be converted to roll-on roll-off operation. Linkspans, end-loading at Wemyss Bay and set into the face of the pier at Rothesay, were introduced in 1977. On 30th June of that year the *Saturn* was launched by Mrs I S Irwin, wife of CalMac's Chairman. She was to be the dedicated Rothesay ferry, replacing the *Glen Sannox*. She suffered, however, from problems associated with the alignment of her shafts and was unable to enter service until 2nd February 1978. Her difficulties continued through her first season but were then completely rectified. Although marginally slower than her two quasi-sisters *Jupiter* and *Juno,* she did incorporate several improvements, notably a high-level bridge, a tripod mainmast rather than the tetrapod mast of the original pair and a different form of hull, to cope better with the more exposed Rothesay crossing.

Originally designated 'ROTHESAY FERRY' – just as her sisters bore the legend 'GOUROCK-DUNOON FERRY' – the *Saturn*, like her consorts, was instead given the CalMac logo in 1984. This change was timely as from 1986 she interchanged with the *Jupiter* and *Juno*. One ship would serve Dunoon, the second Rothesay while the third was allocated to the 'No 1A Roster', which comprised MoD sailings to Kilcreggan (until 1995), peak sailings to Dunoon and additional morning runs to Rothesay. Gradually the Wemyss Bay-Rothesay route became the busiest in the CalMac network so that, by 2003, two ships were allocated to it throughout the year. When the *Bute* appeared in 2005, the *Saturn* found a new role as a backup to the *Caledonian Isles* on the Ardrossan-Brodick route, because of the ever-increasing freight traffic. Outwith the main season, she returns to the Upper Firth, as relief vessel and stand-by. The *Saturn* became the only vessel of her type to have left the Clyde when in September 2007 she sailed to Islay for berthing trials.

Ardrossan - Brodick (summer)
Spare vessel (winter)

Miles Cowsill

Gross tons	851
Length	69.5m
Breadth	13.8m
Draught	2.45m
Maximum Passenger Capacity	531
Vehicles	38
Builders	Ailsa Shipbuiding Co Ltd, Troon
Built	1978
Speed	12 knots
Retail Area	Coffee Cabin

Saturn (Dave Wolstenhome)

ISLE OF ARRAN
Eilean Arainn

Kennacraig - Port Ellen & Port Askaig (Islay)

On the route from Ardrossan to Brodick, Arran, in the early 1980s, the summer ferry *Clansman* lacked speed and manoeuvrability and the winter ferry *Caledonia* capacity. Their replacement, the *Isle of Arran*, was launched on 2nd December 1983 by Miss Joanna Younger, daughter of Scotland's Secretary of State. Sailing at 15 knots, she performed the service in the allotted 55 minutes and her winter passenger complement was more than adequate. She took up the run on 13th April 1984 and was an immediate success.

With a small open area at the stern, the *Isle of Arran* looked aesthetically pleasing, especially after her first season when the white paint on her superstructure was lowered. In 1998 she had the black paint at her bow stepped up to the original height. She has two observation lounges on the boat deck forward, one doubling as a bar, while aft is a spacious cafeteria. The accommodation was extensively refurbished in 1990. The *Isle of Arran* was the first CalMac ferry to have an invalid lift from car deck to passenger lounge.

A larger vessel, the *Caledonian Isles*, was commissioned for the Arran service in 1993 and the 'Arran' became the designated Islay ferry – largely based at Kennacraig and normally sailing alternately to Port Ellen and Port Askaig. In winter, she became CalMac's spare vessel and by the end of her first season on this duty she had sailed on all the major CalMac routes bar one (Mallaig-Armadale).

On the commissioning of the *Hebrides* in 2001, the *Hebridean Isles* was transferred to Islay and the *Isle of Arran* became spare. After a spell as secondary vessel on the Stornoway-Ullapool station, she gave extra sailings out of Oban in the 2002 season but since 2003 she has returned to Islay as second vessel in an enhanced service, a feature which is now permanent. A purpose-built ship is due to replace the *Isle of Arran* at Islay in 2011.

Lawrence Macduff

Gross tons	3,269
Length	84.9m
Breadth	15.8m
Draught	3.2m
Maximum Passenger Capacity	659
Vehicles	62
Builders	Ferguson Ailsa Ltd, Port Glasgow
Built	1984
Speed	15 knots
Retail Area	Coffee Cabin
	Mariners Cafeteria

Isle of Arran (Graham Wilson)

HEBRIDEAN ISLES
Eileanan Innse Gall

The first car ferry route to be established by MacBrayne's was the 'Uig triangle' between Uig (Skye) and Tarbert (Harris) and Lochmaddy (North Uist). For over twenty years from its inauguration in 1964, the route had been entrusted to the pioneer hoist-loading car ferry *Hebrides*. Agreement was eventually reached to convert the route to ro-ro operation. Cochrane's of Selby offered the best value contract and the *Hebridean Isles*, complete with bow and stern ramp and hoist, was duly launched on 4th July 1985. She was the first CalMac vessel to be named by royalty – in her case HRH The Duchess of Kent. Her passenger facilities resemble those of the *Isle of Arran*, but she set new standards in this regard.

The *Hebridean Isles* was delivered late in 1985 but because none of the linkspans she required was ready she spent her first winter based first at Stornoway and then at Oban. In May 1986 she was able to appear on her dedicated route and eventually a full ro-ro service commenced. Even greater efficiency resulted from the commissioning of the *Loch Bhrusda* on the Sound of Harris run a decade later, the *Hebridean Isles* then being able to omit the Lochmaddy-Tarbert leg.

After fifteen years of sterling service the *Hebridean Isles* was replaced by the larger *Hebrides* in 2001. She was transferred to the Islay run from Kennacraig, in most seasons with a weekly run to Colonsay and Oban, initially on her own but then partnered by the *Isle of Arran*. She was absent, however, for six months from October 2002 when she was chartered by NorthLink to inaugurate their Stromness-Scrabster service until the pierworks at Scrabster were complete. She returned north for a short spell on relieving duties each winter. This practice ceased in 2007 as the new contract with the Government meant that a vessel leased from CMAL to one subsidiary company could no longer be chartered to another.

Kennacraig - Port Ellen & Port Askaig (Islay) with weekly summer extension to Colonsay and Oban

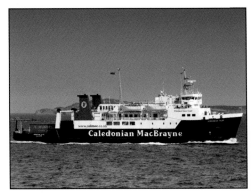

Dave Wolstenholme

Gross tons	3,040
Length	85.2m
Breadth	15.8m
Draught	3.11m
Maximum Passenger Capacity	494
Vehicles	62
Builders	Cochrane Shipbuilders Ltd, Selby, North Yorkshire
Built	1985
Speed	15 knots
Retail Area	Coffee Cabin
	Mariners Cafeteria
	Shop@CalMac

Hebridean Isles (John Newth)

ISLE OF MULL
An t-Eilean Muileach

The traffic between Oban and Craignure in Mull had increased to such an extent by the mid-1980s that a new larger vessel had to be ordered. Launched on 8th December 1987, she was named *Isle of Mull* by HRH Princess Alexandra – but while she was being fitted out news broke that she had a serious deadweight problem. Despite being perfectly safe and having unsurpassed accommodation, her carrying capacity fell far short of specification. She did indeed enter service on 11th April 1988, in all other aspects with complete success. She was taken off the run, however, for two months in October to be lengthened by 5.4 metres, at the builder's expense, in order to cure the problem. She was cut in two immediately forward of the funnel and had a prefabricated section successfully fitted in drydock at Middlesbrough on the Tees. The passenger accommodation on the *Isle of Mull* is of a very high standard with a spacious cafeteria with two serveries forward and a very comfortable bar area aft. An observation lounge with panoramic windows is a feature of the deck above. At the stern there is a remarkable amount of open deck space with fixed seating.

With a complement of 80 cars and, in summer, 1,000 passengers, capacity problems on the busy Mull crossing were solved at a stroke. Traffic has continued to grow, however, with a huge variety of excursions incorporating her sailings, and her roster has had to be slackened to allow greater turnaround times. The *Isle of Mull* occasionally deviates from her own run if traffic so requires and she has relieved at Stornoway and even Brodick, Arran. With a linkspan installed on the island, the Mull ferry was able to include Colonsay in her roster. Since 2003, however, an extra seasonal ferry based at Oban covers Colonsay in summer, and so the *Isle of Mull* can concentrate purely on the Craignure route.

Oban - Craignure (Mull)
(+Colonsay in winter)

John Hendy

Gross tons	4,719
Length	90.03m
Breadth	15.8m
Draught	3.19m
Maximum Passenger Capacity	951
Vehicles	70
Builders	Appledore Ferguson Shipbuilders Ltd, Port Glasgow
Built	1988
Speed	15 knots
Retail Area	Coffee Cabin
	Mariners Cafeteria
	The Still
	Shop@CalMac

Isle of Mull (Alan Neil)

LORD OF THE ISLES
Rìgh nan Eilean

In the late 1980s traffic out of Oban was far less than now and so both the Tiree ferry *Columba* and the Outer Isles ferry *Claymore* could be replaced by one vessel. A new ship was duly launched on 7th March 1989 and named *Lord of the Isles* by Mrs Edith Rifkind, wife of the then Secretary of State for Scotland. The accommodation is of a high specification. The *Lord of the Isles*, affectionately known as '*LOTI*',was the last vessel in the fleet to have sleeping accommodation, although this has not been used in recent years. Her vehicle deck is open at the stern to allow the carriage of dangerous goods. Recently, following minimal modification, passengers were for the first time allowed on her upper deck, with the attendant spectacular views, while her bar lounge has been redesigned to incorporate a coffee cabin and shop.

When the *Lord of the Isles* first took up service, on 22nd May 1989, only three of her ports of call had linkspans and so she had to be designed with a hoist. She sailed seven days a week, sometimes through the night, juggling six trips weekly to Barra and South Uist with four to Coll and Tiree. Her schedule did become less arduous with the introduction of linkspans at Coll and Tiree in 1992. She was at the time the fastest vessel in the fleet, with a service speed of over 16 knots. In July 1998 the larger *Clansman* took over and '*LOTI*' was transferred to the seasonal Mallaig-Armadale station in lieu of the *Iona*. Until 2001, however, she continued to serve Castlebay and Lochboisdale overnight from Mallaig, and returned to her old haunts each winter as her successor was CalMac's relief vessel. In 2003 she was replaced and returned to her Oban base permanently to partner the *Clansman*, serving in addition Colonsay and even Islay, while for four years she offered special excursions to places like Tobermory.

Oban-Coll,Tiree; Oban- Castlebay (Barra), Lochboisdale (South Uist)
(+Colonsay in summer)

Lawrence Macduff

Gross tons	3,504
Length	84.6m
Breadth	15.8m
Draught	3.19m
Maximum Passenger Capacity	506
Vehicles	54
Builders	Appledore Ferguson Shipbuilders Ltd, Port Glasgow
Built	1989
Speed	16 knots
Retail Area	Coffee Cabin
	Mariners Cafeteria

Lord of the Isles (Dave Wolstenholme)

CALEDONIAN ISLES
Eileanan Chaledonia

Ardrossan - Brodick (Arran)

The *Caledonian Isles* appeared in 1993. It had been realised for some time that the *Isle of Arran*, purpose-built for the Ardrossan-Brodick route less than a decade previously, was proving inadequate and motorists and commercial carriers were often unable to obtain the bookings they wanted. The answer was a larger vessel and a new Arran ferry was duly launched on 25th May 1993 and named by HRH The Princess Royal. When she was ready to enter service, however, a major computer fault occurred and this delayed her first commercial sailing till late August. Further problems developed, her sheer size compared with her predecessor being a factor, especially as her first few months coincided with a spell of boisterous weather when she had often to divert to Gourock, her emergency mainland port. Nevertheless, she soon settled down and became a real boon to the island. The impressive ship has remained a success ever since and has not deviated from her designated station.

An exceptionally roomy vessel with a great deal of open deck space, the *Caledonian Isles* has accommodation far outclassing that of her predecessor. Her upper deck comprises an entrance hall amidships, with a café lounge forward and an area suitable as a snack bar or for more formal dining. Aft of the hall and reception area is a commodious lounge bar while forward on the boat deck above is a fine observation lounge. Refurbishment of the passenger accommodation occurred before the 2004 season.

Even bigger than the *Isle of Mull*, on which she was modelled, the *Caledonian Isles* is the largest ever 'Clyde steamer'. Despite this, since 2005 traffic on the Arran station has been so heavy that the *Saturn* has had to offer a seasonal secondary service on a year-to-year basis. In winter, the *Caledonian Isles* herself, now based all year round at Ardrossan, carries out extra rostered sailings, so that her timetable is virtually the same throughout the year.

Miles Cowsill

Gross tons	5,221
Length	94.0m
Breadth	15.8m
Draught	3.2m
Maximum Passenger Capacity	1,000
Vehicles	110
Builders	Richards (Shipbuilders) Ltd, Lowestoft, Suffolk
Built	1993
Speed	15 knots
Retail Area	Coffee Cabin
	Mariners Cafeteria
	The Still
	Shop@CalMac

Caledonian Isles (Dave Wolstenholme)

www.calmac.co.uk

CALEDONIAN ISLES
GLASGOW

Eileanan Chaledonia

CALEDONIAN ISLES

Caledonian MacBrayne

ISLE OF LEWIS
Eilean Leòdhais

One of CalMac's most prestigious routes is the 'marine motorway' between Ullapool and Stornoway. Since 1974 the service had been entrusted to the *Suilven*, a steady and reliable ship from Norway whose speed and accommodation left a little to be desired. Her Clyde-built replacement was launched on 18th April 1995 and named *Isle of Lewis* by HRH Princess Alexandra. On trials she reached a speed of 18.92 knots, making her the fastest ever motor vessel in the fleet of CalMac or its predecessors. She is even longer than the *Caledonian Isles* and her gross tonnage too is considerably greater. Her accommodation, which has recently been refurbished, is truly spacious and one can stand aft of the bar on the promenade deck and look right forward through the passenger concourse with its varied facilities to the cafeteria. She also has ample open deck space.

The new ferry took up service on 31st July 1995 and eventually settled down to a passage time of a mere 2 hours 45 minutes. A new roster was devised – on certain days three double runs were offered and so, for the first time, a day excursion was offered from Ullapool to Stornoway.

As a result of competition in 2001, the *Isle of Lewis* added a nightly cargo run to her own roster. A freight vessel was eventually chartered for the overnight service and the *Isle of Lewis* returned to her normal timetable.

For many years she was the only major ferry in the fleet not to sail seven days per week, due to the traditional observance of the Sabbath in Lewis. Following intensive discussions, however, she sailed on a scheduled service on a Sunday for the first time on 19th July 2009.

In 2009 the *Isle of Lewis* became the first CalMac vessel to be surveyed outwith the UK – at Fredericia in Denmark.

G.Wilson

Gross tons	6,753
Length	101.25m
Breadth	18.52m
Draught	4.19m
Maximum Passenger Capacity	970
Vehicles	114
Builders	Ferguson Shipbuilders Ltd, Port Glasgow
Built	1995
Speed	18 knots
Retail Area	Coffee Cabin
	Mariners Cafeteria
	The Still
	Shop@CalMac

Isle of Lewis (Dave Wolstenholme)

CLANSMAN
Fear-cinnidh

Traffic had increased so much on the Islands run from Oban by the mid-1990s that a replacement for the *Lord of the Isles* had become essential. In addition the ferry on the Mallaig-Armadale route, the *Iona* of 1970, did not conform to the latest stringent safety regulations, the 'LOTI' being an obvious successor. A product of Devon, the new Oban vessel *Clansman* was the first of the new breed of ships to revert to a traditional name, given to her by HRH The Princess Royal on 27th March 1998. She was designed to carry 90 cars and to be the maximum size of ship able to operate safely and efficiently to the island terminals. It was 4th July before she was able to enter service and emergency arrangements had to be made to fill the gap in the fleet as the *Iona* had already been sold.

The *Clansman* is an imposing vessel and indeed quite dwarfed her predecessor. The after end of her car deck has been left open so that she can carry dangerous cargoes; her bow is round and massive. Her passenger accommodation is on two levels with a full-width cafeteria forward and lounge bar aft on the promenade deck. One deck up is an observation lounge where the seating is particularly comfortable as, unlike the *Lord of the Isles*, she has no sleeping berths and, at least initially, she was rostered for overnight sailings. When new, she lacked open deck space but this was partially remedied for the 2004 season with the extension of her boat deck aft of the funnel. With a speed of over 16 knots, the *Clansman* is able to cope with her demanding roster. For the first four years, she alone served Coll, Tiree, Barra and South Uist from Oban in summer, while in winter she became CalMac's main relief vessel. Since 2002 she has shared the Oban traffic, mainly with the *Lord of the Isles*.

Oban-Coll, Tiree; Oban- Castlebay (Barra), Lochboisdale (South Uist)
Relief Vessel in winter

Colin Smith

Gross tons	5,499
Length	99.0m
Breadth	16.28m
Draught	3.22m
Maximum Passenger Capacity	638
Vehicles	90
Builders	Appledore Shipbuilders Ltd, Bideford, Devon
Built	1998
Speed	16.5 knots
Retail Area	Coffee Cabin
	Mariners Cafeteria
	Shop@CalMac

Clansman (Alan Neill)

47

LOCHNEVIS
Loch Nibheis

The Small Isles – Eigg, Muck, Rum and Canna – are served from Mallaig. Until 2004 only Canna possessed a pier while at the others traffic had to be landed by flitboat. From July 1979 the ship on the station had been the rather small *Lochmor*. Extensive consultation was promised to find the best design and way of working for a replacement ship. With EU financial help, each of the Small Isles was to be given an appropriate slipway although in the interim period the new ship would have to load and unload in the time-honoured way and she would also have to use the linkspan at Mallaig. The *Lochnevis* was duly launched at Troon on 8th May 2000 and named by Transport Minister Sarah Boyack, MSP. The electronic gadgetry in her engine room and navigating bridge, her spacious passenger accommodation and huge stern ramp all made her quite a remarkable vessel.

Due to the sophistication of her machinery and the fact that the yard closed soon after her launch date, fitting out took longer than anticipated and it was 20th November before the *Lochnevis* entered service, following trials on the Clyde. Her superior speed of 13 knots allows day trips with time ashore to be offered. Private boats tendered at Muck and Rum but at Eigg, CalMac provided the flitboat. The *Ulva*, last of the MacBrayne red boats, was worn out and withdrawn to be replaced by a new-build from Corpach, the *Laig Bay*. After protracted delays, with one contractor going into receivership, the promised slipways at Rum, Eigg and Muck were eventually all in place by Easter 2004 and tendering ceased. Canna too received a slipway, adjacent to its traditional pier, in 2006, as did Inverie in Loch Nevis. The *Lochnevis's* most original voyages occurred in 2009 when, under charter, she sailed on separate occasions to South Uist and Barra, together with a unique non-landing cruise to the uninhabited island of Mingulay.

Mallaig - Small Isles (Eigg, Muck, Rum and Canna).
(+Armadale (Skye) in winter)

Dave Wolstenholme

Gross tons	941
Length	49.0m
Breadth	11.4m
Draught	2.7m
Maximum Passenger Capacity	190
Vehicles	16
Builders	Ailsa Shipbuiding Co Ltd, Troon
Built	2000
Speed	13 knots
Retail Area	Coffee Cabin

Lochnevis (Dave Wolstenholme)

Loch Nibheis

www.calmac.co.uk

Caledonian MacBrayne

LOCHNEVIS

HEBRIDES
Innse Gall

Uig (Skye) - Tarbert (Harris)/Lochmaddy (North Uist)

The announcement of the replacement for the *Hebridean Isles* on the Tarbert/Lochmaddy-Uig service was made in July 1998. On 2nd August 2000 the new ship was ready for launching on the Clyde, and was named *Hebrides* by HM The Queen, the first time a reigning monarch had christened a vessel of the company or any of its predecessors. Following fitting out she was given the bell of the first *Hebrides* of 1898 which had also graced the second '*Heb*', MacBrayne's first car ferry dating from 1964.

The design of the new ship was based on that of the *Clansman*, with various improvements suggested by three years of operation. The main distinguishing feature is that her funnel is not obstructed by lifeboats, as her evacuation system is more sophisticated. The 'Eiders Restaurant' and 'Chieftain Bar' especially are furnished to a particularly high standard. Like her quasi-sister, open deck space was improved during her overhaul in early 2004.

The *Hebrides* made her first commercial sailing on 24th March 2001, when capacity on the route was instantly increased by 50%. Since she was appreciably faster than her predecessor, her advent allowed for shorter passage times and so the Uig roster was recast, with three double runs being possible in a twelve-hour period. She berths overnight alternately at Tarbert and Lochmaddy and in the peak summer season two double runs are on offer on Sundays to the latter. Grand Tours of North Uist, the Sound of Harris and the island of Harris itself are run from Uig (in connection with the *Loch Portain*) and are highly popular.

The *Hebrides* has occasionally had to make use in emergency of the terminals at Ullapool and Lochboisdale. In April 2007, following her overhaul and conversion to burn intermediate fuel oil – a substantially cheaper fuel – she was to be found for a week on the Islands run from Oban, which brought her for the first time to Coll, Tiree and Barra.

Lawrence Macduff

Gross tons	5,506
Length	99.0m
Breadth	15.8m
Draught	3.3m
Maximum Passenger Capacity	612
Vehicles	98
Builders	Ferguson Shipbuilders Ltd, Port Glasgow
Built	2000
Speed	16.5 knots
Retail Area	Coffee Cabin
	Mariners Cafeteria
	Shop@CalMac

Hebrides (Dave Wolstenholme)

CORUISK
Coir' Uisg'

Mallaig-Armadale (Skye) Summer
Wemyss Bay - Rothesay reliefs in winter

In October 2001 funding was announced for a 'sheltered waters vessel' to operate the Mallaig-Armadale route in summer and relieve in the Upper Clyde in winter. The result was the *Coruisk*, launched in Devon without ceremony on 3rd May 2003. In some ways resembling the *Loch Portain*, she is very tall relative to her length - this is necessary to comply with new safety regulations which insist that her car deck is higher above the water than those of the older vessels in the fleet, coupled with the necessity for maximum clearance for HGVs below the upper deck. Her open upper deck is substantial and her saloon, with coffee bar-cum-shop, spacious. Beneath is a gallery deck where a gangway gate was later cut into her shell-plating. Two engine uptakes are placed at each end of the upper deck on the starboard side. Originally white, they were soon repainted as CalMac funnels.

Having run speed trials in Devon, the *Coruisk* carried out berthing trials on the Clyde before sailing north to Mallaig. She was formally commissioned on 14th August 2003 and named by Baroness Michie. Her early service, however, was plagued by technical problems culminating in a computer failure which caused her to ground and damage one of her propulsion units. She subsequently sailed for the Clyde and the *Pioneer*, which had been deputising for her, had hurriedly to return.

After extensive repairs, modifications and trials, the ship relieved at Dunoon in November but her debut was rather unfortunate, partly because she was unable to berth at Dunoon Pier at all states of the tide. Her spell on the Rothesay route for a month in early 2004, however, was more successful and when she returned to Mallaig at Easter her problems were behind her. Since then she has settled down to become a stalwart member of the fleet, serving Skye in summer and Bute in winter - when not laid up in Glasgow's King George V Dock.

Dave Wolstenholme

Gross tons	1,559
Length	65.0m
Breadth	14.0m
Draught	3.05m
Maximum Passenger Capacity	249
Vehicles	40
Builders	Appledore Shipbuilders Ltd, Bideford, Devon
Built	2003
Speed	14 knots
Retail Area	Coffee Cabin
	Shop@CalMac

Coruisk (Dave Wolstenholme)

BUTE
Eilean Bhòid

At the start of the new millennium, the Clyde 'streakers' – *Jupiter*, *Juno* and *Saturn* – were well over twenty years old and, although they had given yeoman service, they were coming to the end of their useful lives. In October 2003 it was announced that up to £8.75 million would be made available for a new dedicated ferry for the Wemyss Bay-Rothesay route. It was in March 2004 that the contract for the new vessel was awarded to the yard which had produced what was regarded as the lowest tender out of eight, from Gdansk in Poland.

The new ship was formally handed over to CalMac on 22nd June 2005. Just over 24 hours later she was on her way to the Clyde, diverted via the English Channel on account of severe weather. She was named *Bute* at Rothesay on 1st July by Mrs Marjorie Bulloch, wife of the Depute Lord Lieutenant of Argyll and Bute. Within six months the regular travellers to and from Rothesay really appreciated the asset they had been given, after a few teething problems had been resolved. The *Bute*'s accommodation, her open deck space and, following a slight slackening of the timetable and a bedding-in period, her reliability won over the hearts of the Brandanes, while her capacity was more than sufficient for any traffic flows, even at the busiest periods.

Her first winter in service saw some very stormy weather and she coped remarkably well. From early November 2005 the service was for a while completely in the hands of the new generation of ferries, the *Coruisk* having joined her younger consort. The *Bute* is slightly longer than the 'streakers', and beamier too. Of more conventional appearance than the *Coruisk*, she too features bow and stern loading as well as having a ramp near the stern on the starboard side, required as the end-loading linkspan at Rothesay was not in place until December 2007.

Wemyss Bay - Rothesay (Bute)

Miles Cowsill

Gross tons	2,612
Length	72.0m
Breadth	6.4m
Draught	3.0m
Maximum Passenger Capacity	200
Vehicles	60
Builders	Stocznia Remontowa, Gdansk, Poland
Built	2005
Speed	14 knots
Retail Area	Coffee Cabin
	Shop@CalMac

Bute (Graham Wilson)

ARGYLE
Earra-Ghaidheal

Wemyss Bay - Rothesay (Bute)

The sister ship to the *Bute*, promised for the Wemyss Bay-Rothesay route, was ordered in August 2005. As with the earlier ship, the *Argyle* was built in Gdansk, Poland, in accordance with EU procurement regulations. Like the *Bute*, she is the seventh ship on the Clyde to be so called. The old spelling is appropriate as her most prominent ancestor was the paddle steamer *Argyle* (1866) which sailed from Wemyss Bay for over a quarter of a century.

The new *Argyle* was launched on 12th September 2006 but fitting out took some time and it was 18th April 2007 before she was handed over to CalMac. After voyaging to the Clyde via the English Channel, she was named off Rothesay by Mrs Tish Timms, wife of the Chairman of CalMac Ferries Ltd, on 4th May, before she displaced the elderly *Saturn*. Unlike the *Saturn* which has Voith-Schneider units, the main engines of the *Argyle* and *Bute* drive Schottel rudder propellers fore and aft.

With the new end-loading linkspan at Rothesay still not available at the time, the *Argyle* sports a side ramp. Her main covered passenger space comprises a central free-flow catering area with lounge seats fore and aft, while behind the saloon is a sheltered area outside. The open deck above is spacious. The sisters can be told apart by the arrangement of their windows on the bridge and after saloon, the latter being the result of the new ship's having two passenger lifts from car deck to passenger accommodation, the older vessel only having one. Lifts are required for the mobility-impaired as the passenger accommodation is situated above rather than forward of the car deck (as had been the case in the 'streakers'), sufficient clearance for high vehicles being necessary.

With the arrival of the *Argyle*, and the completion of full end-loading facilities in December 2007, the islanders on Bute could look forward to a service rivalling any in the network.

Lawrence Macduff

Gross tons	2,612
Length	72.0m
Breadth	6.4m
Draught	3.0m
Maximum Passenger Capacity	450
Vehicles	60
Builders	Stocznia Remontowa, Gdansk, Poland
Built	2007
Speed	14 knots
Retail Area	Coffee Cabin
	Shop@CalMac

ISLE OF CUMBRAE
Eilean Chumraigh

Tarbert (Loch Fyne) - Portavadie (Cowal) in summer

By 1976 the service between Largs and Cumbrae Slip (with coach connection to Millport) had been operating for four years. The small elderly vessels, *Coruisk* and *Largs*, were no longer fit for purpose. One large ferry was the answer and the appropriately-named *Isle of Cumbrae* was launched at Troon on 22nd December 1976. Cumbrae Slip was extended and the area round Largs Pier dredged although the old boats were kept in a spare and relief capacity for a few years. In addition, the small ferry *Keppel* was retained for nine years on a passenger-only service from Largs direct to the Old Pier at Millport.

In 1986 the first of the new 'Loch' class ferries appeared and displaced the *Isle of Cumbrae* from her eponymous route. She was transferred to the West Highlands and became the dedicated ferry on the Lochaline-Fishnish (Mull) crossing, thus trebling capacity on the route. Her wheelhouse was originally white but early in 1987 it was repainted red and black like the new 'Lochs' which had replaced her. For some time each winter until 1995 she relieved the Skye ferries at Kyle of Lochalsh.

By the mid-nineties the *Isle of Cumbrae* was having difficulty in accommodating the largest of the commercials regularly using the 'back door' to Mull. A replacement, the *Loch Alainn*, was commissioned on the route in July 1997 and the *Isle of Cumbrae* returned to the Clyde – on the Colintraive-Rhubodach service. She again increased capacity on the route, this time by 50%. A further cascade of vessels took place on the recommissioning of the larger *Loch Dunvegan* on the Kyles run in March 1999. The *Isle of Cumbrae* moved to Tarbert to become the regular ferry, at least in summer, on the Portavadie roster, and has remained on that station, although she carries out some relief work in winter and has seen service over the years at Lismore, Raasay and Kilchoan, in addition to Largs and Lochaline.

Dave Wolstenholme

Gross tons	201
Length	32.0m
Breadth	10.0m
Draught	1.4m
Maximum Passenger Capacity	139
Vehicles	18
Builders	Ailsa Shipbuiding Co Ltd, Troon
Built	1977
Speed	8.5 knots

Isle of Cumbrae (Miles Cowsill)

LOCH STRIVEN
Loch Sroigheann

By the mid-1980s traffic had built up on some of CalMac's minor routes to such an extent that the fleet of 'Island' class vessels dating from the early seventies could not cope and there were still some bow-loaders in the fleet which were even older. In July 1985 two new ferries able to carry twelve cars and 200 passengers were ordered for delivery the following summer. The first of the pair, the *Loch Striven*, was launched on 8th May 1986 and, after fitting out, sailed from the Humber round to Scotland via the Caledonian Canal to take up service between Largs and Cumbrae on 4th July. Fitted with Voith-Schneider propellers, she has two lanes on her car deck, each able to accommodate six cars, while passenger accommodation is provided on each side, with seating also on her open upper decks. An interesting feature is that her wheelhouse on the starboard side is painted as if it were a CalMac funnel.

Initially the *Loch Striven* sailed along with the *Isle of Cumbrae* to give a fifteen-minute interval service but soon she was joined by her sister *Loch Linnhe*. She remained closely associated with Cumbrae for eleven years, although she also happened to be the first 'Loch' on the Kyles of Bute crossing and the winter run from Tarbert to Portavadie and Lochranza.

In 1997 her sister *Loch Riddon* became available for service at Largs. As her ramps operated more quickly, it was decided that she would be more suitable as Cumbrae ferry: the *Loch Striven* was transferred to the West Highlands and on 28th July she displaced the 'Island' class ferry *Raasay* from the Raasay-Sconser route. This was indeed fortuitous as at the time there was a great deal of timber movement from Raasay to Skye and the small ferry had been overwhelmed. She has remained there ever since, Sunday sailings being offered for the first time in 2004.

Caledonian MacBrayne

Gross tons	206
Length	35.0m
Breadth	10.0m
Draught	1.5m
Maximum Passenger Capacity	200
Vehicles	12
Builders	Richard Dunston (Hessle) Ltd, Hessle, East Yorkshire
Built	1986
Speed	9 knots

Loch Striven (Dave Wolstenholme)

61

LOCH LINNHE
An Linne Dhubh

The second of the new vessels known as the 'Loch' class was launched on 22nd May 1986 and, like her elder sister, made her way to the west coast of Scotland via the Caledonian Canal. Although destined for the Clyde, she interrupted her voyage in the Sound of Mull when, on 4th July, she took over from the 'Island' class ferry *Canna* on the run from Lochaline to Fishnish (Mull), giving a much-needed boost to capacity there. A month later she and the *Isle of Cumbrae* changed places and she took up her intended place on the Largs-Cumbrae service.

For over a decade she and the *Loch Striven* continued as the mainstays of the Cumbrae service. In 1997, however, the latter was transferred to Raasay and her place taken by the former Kyles of Bute ferry *Loch Riddon*. A year later the *Loch Linnhe* herself was moved to Tarbert, sailing across Loch Fyne to Portavadie, replacing the 'Island' class vessel *Bruernish* and allowing drive-through operation. In October 1998 the Tarbert-Portavadie route became part of CalMac's undertaking with the Government and so it could be operated on a year-round basis. In winter the ferry on the run would also transport vehicles and dangerous goods to Arran on a midday Tarbert-Lochranza sailing.

Meanwhile, the slipways at Tobermory and Kilchoan were being widened and in April 1999 the *Loch Linnhe* was able to take over the then seasonal service across the Sound of Mull. [She and the *Loch Riddon* changed places in 2000 and so the *Loch Linnhe* returned to Largs for one year.] Before taking up her Kilchoan roster in 2003, she opened the CalMac service between Barra and Eriskay and returned there each spring until 2006 in a relieving capacity. Her current winter role is one of general relief, principally serving Raasay, Gigha, Kilchoan and the Sound of Barra before she returns to the Sound of Mull in the spring.

Tobermory (Mull) - Kilchoan (Ardnamurchan)
Reliefs in winter

Caledonian MacBrayne

Gross tons	206
Length	30.2m
Breadth	10.0m
Draught	1.5m
Maximum Passenger Capacity	200
Vehicles	12
Builders	Richard Dunston (Hessle) Ltd, Hessle, East Yorkshire
Built	1986
Speed	9 knots

Loch Linnhe (Dave Wolstenholme)

LOCH RIDDON
Loch Raodain

A second pair of 'Loch' class ferries was ordered soon after the first. One was ready to be named on 19th August 1986, the ceremony carried out by Mrs Montgomery, the widow of a former CalMac Traffic Manager. The *Loch Riddon* stuck on the launching slip and only entered the water a fortnight later. After a stormy passage round the north of Scotland she reached the Oban area and was pressed into service on 28th October on the Lochaline-Fishnish crossing. It was not long, however, before she was relieved and was able to take her place on the 'back door' service to Bute, from Colintraive in the Cowal peninsula across the narrowest part of the Kyles of Bute to Rhubodach.

The *Loch Riddon* remained at Colintraive for over a decade until she was replaced by the larger *Isle of Cumbrae* in 1997. She then moved to Largs and became the dedicated Cumbrae ferry in partnership with her sister *Loch Linnhe*, replacing her other sister *Loch Striven*, as her ramps operated faster and this was a decided advantage at Largs. In peak season, there were timetabled runs across the Largs Channel every fifteen minutes during most of the day but in winter crossings were less frequent and the *Loch Riddon* was not required when the larger *Loch Alainn* was the main ferry and she could cope on her own. This allowed the *Loch Riddon* to undertake relief work. She was often on the new winter run between Tarbert and Portavadie with a daily trip to Lochranza and in 1999 she ventured into Western Isles territory for the first time. The year 2000 was the only year in which she spent the summer there - on the Tobermory-Kilchoan service. Every other summer she has returned to Largs, since 2003 permanently, as the backup vessel, while in winter she continues to serve Tarbert, Portavadie and Lochranza as well as Iona and Lismore.

Largs - Cumbrae Slip (Summer)
Reliefs in winter

John Hendy

Gross tons	206
Length	30.2m
Breadth	10.0m
Draught	1.5m
Maximum Passenger Capacity	200
Vehicles	12
Builders	Richard Dunston (Hessle) Ltd, Hessle, East Yorkshire
Built	1986
Speed	9 knots

Loch Riddon (Colin Smith)

LOCH RANZA
Loch Raonasa

Miles Cowsill

The final member of the original quartet of the 'Loch' class was launched, in darkness, on 17th December 1986 and was named *Loch Ranza*. She was built, as her name suggests, for the route from Lochranza, in the north west of the island of Arran, across the Kilbrannan Sound to Claonaig, directly opposite in the Kintyre peninsula. The 'Island' class vessel *Rhum* which had been providing the service (started in 1972) was much too small for the traffic offering. The *Loch Ranza* entered service in April 1987 and, for a few years at least, was able to cope adequately.

It was in 1992 that the *Loch Ranza* changed from her original to her present employment. With traffic across the Kilbrannan Sound inexorably building up, she had to be replaced by a larger ferry, the *Loch Tarbert*, which entered service in July 1992. The *Loch Ranza* in turn was sent elsewhere to give an enhanced service. She had been promised to Gigha, where the small 'Island' class ferry *Bruernish* was having difficulty in accommodating some of the large vehicles used by the island's farmers. The slipways at Gigha and the mainland terminal at Tayinloan had not been adapted, however, and it was three months before she could take her place on her new station.

She berths overnight at the old steamer pier, known as the South Pier, which is sheltered by the small island of Cara. Sunday crossings were a feature of her roster in summer but in winter they only commenced in 2000. The slipway at Tayinloan is particularly vulnerable to a build up of seaweed following a stormy period of weather and on a few occasions in winter the *Loch Ranza* has had to use the nearby terminal of Kennacraig in emergency. Seldom deviating from her home base, the *Loch Ranza* has been seen in emergency for brief periods at Largs, Lochranza, Colintraive and Tarbert.

Gross tons	206
Length	30.2m
Breadth	10.0m
Draught	1.5m
Maximum Passenger Capacity	200
Vehicles	12
Builders	Richard Dunston (Hessle) Ltd, Hessle, East Yorkshire
Built	1987
Speed	9 knots

Loch Ranza (Dave Wolstenholme)

LOCH DUNVEGAN
Loch Dùnbheagan

Colintraive - Rhubodach (Bute)

The *Loch Dunvegan* was built for the short crossing between Kyle of Lochalsh and Kyleakin in Skye. Twenty years after the arrival of two large end-loading ferries on the route, a bridge across the narrow strait had been agreed to deal with the ever-increasing queues of vehicles. Meanwhile, CalMac was given finance to build two new ships on condition that they would be sold when they became redundant on the completion of the Skye Bridge. The *Loch Dunvegan* was the first of these: she was launched on 15th March 1991 and named by Mrs Marcella Paterson, wife of CalMac's then Managing Director. Meanwhile, to cope with the traffic, 24-hour working on the ferries had been introduced by the time the new ship entered service on 13th May. Her increased capacity was an immediate boon.

It was on 16th October 1995 that the Skye Bridge finally opened; the *Loch Dunvegan* was laid up in Greenock. Despite the agreement to sell the two sisters, no deal was ever sealed. As events turned out, no other unit in the fleet could replace the new *Loch Alainn* on the Sound of Mull crossing after she suffered a serious breakdown.

The *Loch Dunvegan* was quickly reactivated and sailed for Lochaline, taking over the Fishnish service from 19th August 1997, almost two years since she had last been in public service. She herself broke down within a month, however, and had to be towed to the Clyde for repair. The *Loch Dunvegan* remained spare for over a year until at last a dolphin was constructed at Colintraive slipway to allow a substantial vessel to berth alongside. With the works complete in March 1999, the former Skye ferry was able to take her place as the dedicated Colintraive-Rhubodach ferry, this being the only route on which she could sensibly serve. She has remained there, offering a very frequent and successful service on the five-minute crossing.

Lawrence Macduff

Gross tons	549
Length	54.2m
Breadth	13.0m
Draught	1.6m
Maximum Passenger Capacity	200
Vehicles	36
Builders	Ferguson Shipbuilders Ltd, Port Glasgow
Built	1991
Speed	9 knots

Loch Dunvegan (Miles Cowsill)

69

LOCH FYNE
Loch Fine

Lochaline - Fishnish (Mull)

The *Loch Fyne* soon followed her sister into service. Launched on 12th June 1991 and named by Mrs Elizabeth Struthers, wife of CalMac's Chairman, she gave her first commercial sailing on the Kyle-Kyleakin route on 2nd August.

Both the *Loch Dunvegan* and the *Loch Fyne* have considerable covered accommodation. On the starboard side there are two saloon decks and a further partially open deck with a wheelhouse on top painted red with a black top. On the port side, not built up, is a small 'traditional' CalMac funnel which actually houses the engine exhausts. The *Loch Fyne's* large tetrapod masts were originally white but from 1999 they were repainted yellow, like most of the fleet. Capacity problems on the short route 'over the sea to Skye' were solved, at least temporarily. Some even questioned the need for a bridge at all, although others were quick to complain about the noise associated with the ships' working in the middle of the night.

Following the opening of the Skye Bridge in October 1995, the *Loch Fyne*, with her sister, was laid up in Greenock's James Watt Dock and placed on the sale list. Like her sister, a possible sale to Sierra Leone fell through and her eventual reactivation was caused by an emergency. First the *Loch Alainn* and then the *Loch Dunvegan* suffered from major mechanical problems and had to be replaced urgently. The *Loch Fyne* left the dock and sailed to Lochaline to take over the Fishnish roster on 27th September 1997. Here she was an almost instant success, her very large capacity for passengers and vehicles alike endearing her to the travelling public. As a result she has hardly deviated from the roster since, although she has, rather unusually, taken special cargoes to Lismore and the mainland at Corran. She even gave service on the Clyde in November 2006 – on the Colintraive-Rhubodach service while her sister was in drydock.

G.Wilson

Gross tons	549
Length	54.2m
Breadth	13.0m
Draught	1.6m
Maximum Passenger Capacity	200
Vehicles	36
Builders	Ferguson Shipbuilders Ltd, Port Glasgow
Built	1991
Speed	9 knots

Loch Fyne (Dave Wolstenholme)

LOCH BUIE
Loch Buidhe

Fionnphort (Mull) - Iona

At the very end of 1990 the Westminster Government gave permission for CalMac to invite tenders for a new vessel for the ten-minute crossing from Fionnphort, in Mull, to the Sacred Isle of Iona. With the demise of the cruise vessel sailing round Mull from Oban, all the tourists flocking to the island had to travel to Craignure and then continue their journey by coach across Mull. The two 'Island' class vessels on the run were proving inadequate. The new Iona ferry was launched on 24th October 1991 and named *Loch Buie* –the revival of an old MacBrayne name – by Mrs Margaret Martin, wife of a CalMac Director.

Shorter than the original 'Loch' class ferries, she is designed to carry only nine vehicles, and only islanders' cars or commercials at that. On the other hand, her passenger capacity of 250 reflects her main function. There is passenger accommodation on each side of the car deck but her distinguishing feature is a saloon athwartships above the vehicle space, with windows on all sides. As a consequence, it is impossible for a high vehicle to drive straight along the car deck but this is hardly a disadvantage. Her wheelhouse is painted as a funnel but she also has a real small funnel on the port side at the after end of the upper deck.

The new ferry, towering above all other boats in the Sound of Iona, was an instant success and easily carried across the hordes of tourists disgorging from the coaches at Fionnphort. The Sound is susceptible to heavy swells and in winter a landing at the slipway on Iona is sometimes impossible. Overnight, the *Loch Buie* is to be found in a sheltered area known as the Bull Hole not far from the Mull slipway. She has very seldom deviated from her designated station although she has briefly assisted on the Largs-Cumbrae Slip and Tarbert-Portavadie crossings.

G. Wilson

Gross tons	295
Length	30.2m
Breadth	10.0m
Draught	1.6m
Maximum Passenger Capacity	250
Vehicles	9
Builders	James N Miller & Sons Ltd, St Monans, Fife
Built	1992
Speed	9 knots

Loch Buie (Rob Beale)

LOCH TARBERT
Loch an Tairbeirt

Claonaig - Lochranza (Arran)
Reliefs in winter

Dave Wolstenholme

In the early 1990s, the designated ferry on the Kilbrannan Sound crossing, the *Loch Ranza*, was having problems coping at peak periods and long queues were forming. A larger ship was launched as a replacement from the same stable as the Iona ferry *Loch Buie* on 20th February 1992, being named *Loch Tarbert* by CalMac Director Mrs Evelyn Sillars. She has the same dimensions and hull shape as the Iona vessel but her passenger accommodation is enclosed on the starboard side only, an extra lane of vehicles being provided to port. On the port upper deck is quite a sizeable funnel while on the starboard upper deck below the red and black wheelhouse is a narrow deckhouse with four windows. The *Loch Tarbert* was ready for service on 25th July.

With her extra lane, the *Loch Tarbert* is able to deal with the extra traffic on offer and, with up to nine return crossings each way per day, she is able to transport a fair number of vehicles over the 'back door' to Arran. In severe conditions, the *Loch Tarbert* sometimes makes for the more sheltered Tarbert as her mainland port, some 90 minutes away in Loch Fyne. Initially, she had to berth overnight at a buoy in Lochranza but the steamer pier at Lochranza was specially rebuilt as an overnight berth for her in 2003.

The Lochranza-Claonaig service is seasonal and so the *Loch Tarbert* has to find other employment between October and March. During her first winter she relieved at Colintraive and Lochaline, and the second at Iona. Subsequently she became the regular relief vessel at Largs, until the arrival of *Loch Shira* in 2007, and she served on the Sound of Harris between 1997 and 2002. Since 1998 she has also been found on the Tarbert-Portavadie/ Lochranza winter run, especially at the beginning and end of the season, while in 2007 she served Gigha and relieved on the Sound of Barra.

Gross tons	211
Length	30.2m
Breadth	10.0m
Draught	1.6m
Maximum Passenger Capacity	142
Vehicles	17
Builders	James N Miller & Sons Ltd, St Monans, Fife
Built	1992
Speed	9 knots

Loch Tarbert (Miles Cowsill)

Loch an Tairbeirt   www.calmac.co.uk

LOCH TARBERT
GLASGOW

Caledonian MacBrayne

75

LOCH BHRUSDA
Loch Bhrùsta

A coherent link, by bridge, causeway or ferry, had for many years been a dream of the islanders in the Outer Hebrides. In March 1995 this became more of a reality when a vessel was ordered for the route across the Sound of Harris. On 29th March 1996 the new 'Loch' was named *Loch Brusda* by Lady Susan Hamilton. Her wheelhouse is amidships high above the car deck, while her two deckhouses have their outboard sides painted like CalMac funnels. Because the Sound between North Uist and Harris is very shallow in places, CalMac decided to use Schottel pump jet propulsion, with nothing protruding under the vessel's keel. There was quite a delay before the new ferry could enter service as buoys had to be laid to ensure her safe passage in the treacherous waters of the Sound.

On 8th June the *Loch Bhrusda* made a successful debut between Otternish, at the north of North Uist, and Leverburgh, in South Harris. Meanwhile, CalMac, by agreement with Comhairle nan Eilean Siar (Western Isles Council), operated their *Eilean Bhearnaraigh* between Otternish and Berneray Slip, although the *Loch Bhrusda* carried out the sailings herself in winter – until December 1998 when a causeway was completed between North Uist and Berneray and the latter could be used for the Sound of Harris service.

In the meantime, a causeway between South Uist and Eriskay had been built and the Eriskay-Barra crossing would complete the last link in the chain. In 2002 the Comhairle provided such a service; CalMac took over in April 2003 with the *Loch Linnhe* and, as soon as the new *Loch Portain* had replaced her, the *Loch Bhrusda* was able to become the dedicated Sound of Barra ferry. When the larger *Loch Alainn* became available in June 2007, she took over and the *Loch Bhrusda* became spare. In this capacity she has relieved at Cumbrae, Lochranza and the Small Isles and has returned to the Sound of Barra and Sound of Harris.

Dave Wolstenholme

Gross tons	246
Length	35.4m
Breadth	10.88m
Draught	1.4m
Maximum Passenger Capacity	150
Vehicles	18
Builders	McTay Marine, Bromborough, Merseyside
Built	1996
Speed	8 knots

Loch Bhrusda (Dave Wolstenholme)

LOCH ALAINN
Loch Àlainn

Barra - Eriskay

The service across the Sound of Mull from Lochaline to Fishnish commenced in 1973. From 1986 the *Isle of Cumbrae* was on the station but it was found that the lack of covered accommodation on the ageing vessel and the limited space on her car deck were disadvantages. A replacement was ordered in March 1996 and was named *Loch Aline* by Mrs Jill Rankin, wife of the then CalMac Chairman, on 18th April 1997. It was soon discovered, however, that that name was not available and so the Gaelic spelling *Loch Alainn* was used instead. Outwardly the new ship resembled the *Loch Bhrusda* of the previous year, but on a bigger scale. One important difference is that she is propelled by Voith-Schneider propellers.

The *Loch Alainn's* first passenger sailing took place on the Clyde when on 8th July 1997 she was placed in emergency on the Colintraive-Rhubodach service. She did not take up the Sound of Mull run for some time but problems with the Fishnish slipway at low water caused early operational difficulties. A month later, however, she suffered a serious breakdown and had to be towed to the Clyde for repairs. The required spare parts could not be fitted till November and the former Skye ferry *Loch Fyne* was coping successfully at Lochaline. It was decided that the *Loch Alainn* would be of greater use on the Clyde and she returned to Colintraive for three months before taking up service between Largs and Cumbrae Slip in May 1998. This time she was successful and was the mainstay of the Cumbrae service for the following nine years, sailing mainly with the *Loch Riddon* as her consort. In May 2007 she was superseded by the larger *Loch Shira* and was transferred to Barra to replace the *Loch Bhrusda* and solve a capacity problem there. She berths overnight at Ardmhor in Barra and sails to and from the island of Eriska, giving up to five return sailings each day.

Dave Wolstenholme

Gross tons	396
Length	41.0m
Breadth	13.4m
Draught	1.73m
Maximum Passenger Capacity	150
Vehicles	20
Builders	Buckie Shipyard Ltd, Buckie, Banffshire
Built	1997
Speed	10 knots

Loch Alainn (John Hendy)

LOCH PORTAIN
Lochportain

Berneray - Leverburgh (Harris)

In late October 2001 the Scottish Executive announced a large injection of cash into transport infrastructure, funding being provided for a new ferry for the Sound of Harris. The *Loch Bhrusda* had been so successful that a larger vessel was required. Launched without ceremony on 24th March 2003, the new ship, whose hull had been built in Poland, was named *Loch Portain* exactly a month later by Mrs Marion Mills, wife of CalMac's Chairman, and entered service on 5th June. The *Loch Portain* is altogether much larger than her predecessor. Unlike the *Loch Bhrusda*, her passenger accommodation is above the car deck athwartships rather than down one side but like her she has Schottel pump jet propulsion, but neither her exhausts nor any part of the superstructure has been painted to look like a CalMac funnel.

The new ship was an instant success. Unlike some of her consorts, she did not appear to suffer from technical teething problems and the service was disrupted only because of low tide, fog or gales. She continues the well-established practice of taking between North Uist and Harris coach passengers who sail to Lochmaddy on the *Hebrides* and return from Tarbert (or *vice versa*), an exceptionally attractive day excursion.

Navigation in the Sound of Harris is uniquely treacherous even for the West of Scotland and the new ship carefully follows the buoys laid for the *Loch Bhrusda*. She has to avoid sandbanks and rocks and the course between buoys is tortuous, often requiring a swing of more than 90 degrees on passage. One problem that results from this hazardous course is that the *Loch Portain* is not permitted to sail in hours of darkness, with the consequence that her roster has to be changed every few weeks in winter to suit the varying hours of daylight. Since April 2006, she has provided a Sunday service – the first ever to Harris.

Caledonian MacBrayne

Gross tons	950
Length	50.0m
Breadth	14.0m
Draught	1.5m
Maximum Passenger Capacity	195
Vehicles	31
Builders	McTay Marine, Bromborough, Merseyside
Built	2003
Speed	10.5 knots

Loch Portain (Dave Wolstenholme)

LOCH SHIRA
Loch Siora

Largs - Cumbrae

Since the introduction of car ferries between Largs and Cumbrae Slip (which served the town of Millport) in 1972, traffic had increased enormously. Despite ever larger vessels being employed on the route, by 2005 a further increase in capacity and standard of passenger facilities was required, together with an upgrade of the terminal facilities at Largs. On 8th December 2006 a new ship dedicated to the route was launched from Port Glasgow and named *Loch Shira* by Mrs Elspeth Sinclair, wife of the Managing Director of CalMac Ferries Ltd, and witnessed by the public cruising nearby on the *Saturn*. After fitting out and trials, she sailed to the Old Pier at Millport for a very successful Open Day and finally entered service on 2nd June 2007.

The *Loch Shira* is the largest of the 'Loch' class vessels – five metres longer even than the *Loch Portain* on which she was largely modelled. Her sheer size made it prudent for her to lie at Fairlie overnight until the promised extension to Largs Pier was completed by CMAL in late 2009. As in the case of the Sound of Harris ferry, her passenger accommodation extends the full width of the hull above the car deck but in addition she has a passenger lounge at car deck level, a necessary feature on a crossing lasting only ten minutes. Unlike her consort she is propelled by Voith units rather than Schottel pump jets. With a capacity of 250 passengers and 36 cars, it was reckoned at the time of her commissioning that she would be more than adequate for the traffic offering and was likely to remain Cumbrae ferry for many years to come. In the shoulder period at the beginning and end of the summer season, the new ship can cope very well on her own and the ferry on the secondary roster, the *Loch Riddon*, is now seldom required other than in high summer.

Miles Cowsill

Gross tons	1,024
Length	53.9m
Breadth	13.9m
Draught	1.8m
Maximum Passenger Capacity	250
Vehicles	36
Builders	Ferguson Shipbuilders Ltd, Port Glasgow
Built	2007
Speed	10 knots

Loch Shira (Andrew Hickford)

EIGG
Eilean Eige

Oban - Lismore

The oldest survivor of the 'Island' class ferries is the *Eigg*, launched on 12th December 1974. The previous vessels were the *Kilbrannan*, *Morvern*, *Bruernish*, *Rhum* and *Coll*, all products of Port Glasgow. The *Eigg* gave her first passenger sailing in emergency on 25th February 1975 on the crossing between Kyle of Lochalsh and Kyleakin, in the days before the Skye Bridge. A month later she inaugurated the bow-loading service to Raasay from Portree in Skye, replacing the age-old mailboat from Kyle. The *Eigg* remained at Raasay until superseded by her sister *Canna* in early 1976. She then became the Oban-Lismore ferry and has remained at Lismore almost every year since, although she has operated from Largs, Lochranza, Lochaline, Tobermory, Fionnphort and Raasay and to the island of Eigg. She was actually the dedicated Tobermory-Kilchoan ferry between 1996 and 1998 and was also chosen on occasions to bring livestock from the Small Isles to the mainland, often on Sundays when there were no Lismore sailings. Initially she even ran on occasions to Glensanda on the west side of Loch Linnhe with quarry traffic. In the spring she often relieved, on charter, the ferry operating between Port Askaig on Islay and Feolin on Jura. Prior to the winter of 2008/09 she had incorporated into her roster during slack periods calls at Craignure in Mull, with dangerous goods, and Kerrera, the small island off Oban, largely with fish farm traffic. The number of crossings to Lismore has recently increased, and she is now rostered to operate on Sundays.

To conform to new safety regulations whereby the helmsman on the bridge of a vessel has to have an unrestricted view forward, in 1999 the *Eigg*'s wheelhouse was raised a deck. When she is being relieved at Lismore by another 'Island' class vessel, a 'Loch' class has to stand by to transport the high loads offering. The *Eigg* was re-engined in 2001.

Colin Smith

Gross tons	69
Length	22.5m
Breadth	6.4m
Draught	1.4m
Maximum Passenger Capacity	75
Vehicles	5
Builders	James Lamont & Co Ltd, Port Glasgow
Built	1974
Speed	8 knots

Eigg (Dave Wolstenholme)

RAASAY
Eilean Ratharsair

The *Raasay*, launched from Port Glasgow on 23rd March 1976, was the last of the eight 'Island' class ferries to be commissioned. After her first passenger sailings on the Clyde – between Largs and Cumbrae Slip – she sailed for waters more appropriate to her name and on 9th July took over the Raasay-Sconser service from her sister *Canna*. Traffic to and from Raasay was fairly light and so the *Raasay* could give special cargo runs to such remote outposts as Fladda and Rona. She seldom deviated from her island base.

By the late 1990s, however, the *Raasay* was not coping, especially with the timber traffic from the island. In 1997 the 'Loch' class ferry *Loch Striven*, with double her vehicle capacity, became available and took over the service. The *Raasay* became spare vessel, although she did return in a relieving capacity in some winters. That first summer she called at eighteen ports in the course of her duties. Livestock sailings, for example, to the Small Isles were interspersed with periods on the Lismore or Kilchoan rosters. When not in service she frequently lay at a buoy in Tobermory Bay or at Oban. With her hull painted black after her overhaul in 1999, she took over some of the *Eigg*'s relieving duties. When the *Lochnevis* took over the Small Isles run from Mallaig in 2001 the *Raasay* became her regular relief for six years. From 2003 she also replaced her sister *Canna* on the Northern Ireland service between Rathlin and Ballycastle but this task ceased when that contract was given to an Irish operator and the *Canna* was chartered by CMAL to him. Since the 2003/04 winter the *Raasay* has often been found on the winter service between Tobermory and Kilchoan. In 2004, she exchanged places with her older sister *Bruernish* and became the summer relief vessel for the Clyde area. The *Raasay* was the third member of her class to be re-engined, in 2003.

Caledonian MacBrayne

Gross tons	69
Length	22.5m
Breadth	6.4m
Draught	1.4m
Maximum Passenger Capacity	75
Vehicles	5
Builders	James Lamont & Co Ltd, Port Glasgow
Built	1976
Speed	8 knots

Raasay (Dave Wolstenholme)

RAASAY

Caledonian MacBrayne

Eilean Ratharsair   www.calmac.co.uk

MÙIRNEAG

In 2001 opposition appeared on CalMac's Stornoway-Ullapool route in the form of a freight vessel operating an overnight service. Although the experiment was short-lived, it was obvious that there was a demand for such a service, especially from the fishing and seafood industries. Immediately the opposition was withdrawn, CalMac initiated their own overnight cargo run, using the Stornoway ferry *Isle of Lewis*. Largely because of crew considerations, this service was difficult to sustain and another ferry, initially the *Lord of the Isles* but subsequently the *Isle of Arran*, was drafted in to assist. The best option, however, was for the company to charter a freight vessel for the night service and allow the *Isle of Lewis* to return to her normal roster. Initially NorthLink's *Hascosay* was employed but from October 2002 she was required in the Northern Isles and a replacement had to be found. The *Belard* was chosen.

This 1979 Danish-built cargo ship, originally named *Mercandian Carrier II*, was rechristened first *Alianza* and then *Carrier II*. In 1985 she passed to P&O and received the name *Belard*, appropriately as she operated a trailer service between Belfast and Ardrossan. This was her employment for eight years before she was chartered, and later sold, to the Isle of Man Steam Packet Company, then to a Danish company and finally, in 2002, to Harrisons (Clyde). She is a traditional stern-loading freight ferry with several vehicle decks, accommodation forward and twin funnels, supporting the mainmast, aft.

Following her charter to CalMac, initially for two years but subsequently extended, she retained her Harrisons blue hull but her funnels were repainted in CalMac colours and the company's website address was painted on her upperworks. Soon after arriving in Stornoway on 26th September 2002 she was renamed *Mùirneag* by Mrs Morag MacDonald, wife of the Convener of Comhairle nan Eilean Siar. Her normal departure from Stornoway is just before midnight and she arrives back around 0830.

On charter for Ullapool - Stornoway overnight freight service

Caledonian MacBrayne

Gross tons	5,801
Length	106.0m
Breadth	18.8m
Draught	4.96m
Maximum Passenger Capacity	12
Trailers (max)	54
Builders	Frederikshavn Vaerft A/S Frederikshavn, Denmark
Built	1979
Speed	15 knots

Muirneag (Dave Wolstenholme)

89

ALI CAT

In the early 2000s the Rothesay car ferry left at peak times every 90 minutes whereas at Dunoon, if the rival Western Ferries were included, there were up to five sailings per hour. The third estuarial vessel gave peak commuter runs on the Dunoon station and served Rothesay during the quieter part of the day. CalMac decided that for the 2002/03 winter the third 'streaker' would be transferred full-time to Rothesay and a passenger only vessel chartered to maintain two crossings to and from Dunoon in the morning and one at teatime. This was legitimate as the company's restricted subsidy on the Dunoon run was for passenger services only.

The vessel chosen for the role was the *Ali Cat* (1999), a catamaran of fibreglass and aluminium construction owned by Solent & Wightline Cruises. She has comfortable covered accommodation, including a café bar, and an open deck above for use in fair weather.

The *Ali Cat* took up her roster at the start of the winter timetable on 21st October. When not in service she lies in Greenock's James Watt Dock and sallies forth each morning and evening for Gourock. The site of the Victorian pier at Dunoon is vulnerable to the prevailing southerly swell and some of her services had to be cancelled, leading to some discontent. The construction of a breakwater at Dunoon in 2004, however, has helped berthing enormously and the *Ali Cat* now seldom misses a run.

The *Ali Cat*'s charter was extended to the summer months to allow the fourth Upper Clyde vessel, the *Pioneer*, initially to take over the Skye ferry service and ultimately to be withdrawn from the end of 2003, thus effecting considerable savings. The catamaran has also been used on occasion to supplement sailings between Wemyss Bay and Rothesay at special weekends and has deputised for the main Dunoon ferry in emergency. The *Ali Cat* has also visited Tighnabruaich, Millport and Blairmore on private charters.

Caledonian MacBrayne

Gross tons	99
Length	20.0m
Breadth	8.65m
Draught	1.95m
Maximum Passenger Capacity	250
Builders	South Boats Ltd, East Cowes, Isle of Wight
Built	1999
Speed	14 knots

FINLAGGAN/*Fionn Laggan*
New Build for Kennacraig - Islay

Gross tons	5,209
Length	89.80m
Breadth	16.4m
Draught	3.4m
Maximum Passenger Capacity	550
Vehicles	Approx 88 including mezzanine deck
Builders	Remontawa S.A., Gdansk, Poland
Built	2011
Speed	16 knots

Acknowledgements

CalMac Ferries Ltd would like to thank Ian McCrorie for his valuable work in writing this book, together with Derek Crawford, Harold Mills and John Newth for kindly checking the text. CalMac Ferries Ltd would also like to acknowledge the assistance of Miles Cowsill and all at Ferry Publications for the efforts in bringing this book to fruition. The Company is also grateful to all those who willingly supplied photographs and acknowledges the assistance of the Clyde River and West Highland Steamer Clubs for permission to use their material.

Index of Ships